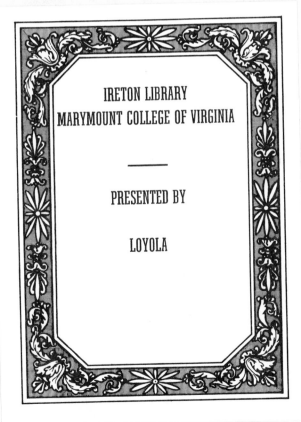

Discovering the
Vernacular Landscape

New London, Connecticut, from the Thames River Bridge. (Photo: Todd Webb)

Discovering the Vernacular Landscape

JOHN BRINCKERHOFF JACKSON

Yale University Press
New Haven and London

We are grateful for permission to reprint with changes the following essays:

"A Puritan Looks at Scenery" from *Landscape Assessment,* ed. Zube, Brush, and Fabos. Copyright © 1975 by Dowden, Hutchinson & Ross, Inc., Stroudsburg, Pa. Originally entitled "A Puritan Views the Landscape."

"The Love of Horizontal Spaces" from the *Annals of the Association of American Geographers,* vol. 62, no. 2, 1972. Originally entitled "Metamorphosis."

"The Movable Dwelling and How It Came to America" from *New Mexico Studies in the Fine Arts,* 1982. Originally entitled "The Mobile Dwelling."

"Craftsman Style and Technostyle" from *VIA,* 1975, a publication of the Graduate School of Fine Arts, University of Pennsylvania. Originally entitled "The Craftsman Style."

"The Origins of Parks" from *Urban Open Spaces,* 1979, a publication of the Cooper-Hewitt Museum, the Smithsonian Institution's National Museum of Design.

"A Vision of New Fields" from *Arts and Architecture,* vol. 1, no. 4, December 1982. Originally entitled "New Fields."

Photographs on pages iii, 38, 56-57, 65, and 83 are from the Standard Oil of New Jersey Collection and are reproduced with permission from the Photographic Archives, University of Louisville.

Designed by Nancy Ovedovitz and set in VIP Galliard type. Printed in the United States of America by Murray Printing Company, Westford, Mass.

Library of Congress Cataloging in Publication Data
Jackson, John Brinckerhoff, 1909–
  Discovering the vernacular landscape.
  Includes bibliographical references and index.
  1. Landscape assessment—United States—Addresses,
essays, lectures.   2. Landscape architecture—United
States—Addresses, essays, lectures.   3. United States—
Description and travel—Addresses, essays, lectures.   I. Title.
GF91.U6J315   1984   304.2'0973   83–21925
ISBN 0–300–03138–6
    0–300–03581–0 (pbk.)

10   9   8   7   6   5   4   3

For Francis Douglas Adams

Contents

Preface

These essays have been selected from a number of lectures I gave during the past ten years. Some have been published in professional journals, but all were originally composed as talks to groups of students and others interested in environmental design: architects and landscape architects and urban planners.

Rereading and editing them for publication as a book has made me uneasily aware that a transcribed lecture is not always a satisfactory literary form. In some ways a lecture resembles an essay: it deals with a single topic from a limited and often highly individual point of view. It is self-contained and it is reasonably short. But whereas the essay can frequently be a work of art, all the more compelling for revealing a colorful personality, a lecture (it has always seemed to me) is simply a way of teaching, of conveying an idea, and nothing more. To be sure, a lecturer who is an entertaining performer as well as one who has something to say is a delight, but a very rare delight. The run-of-the-mill lecturer seeks to enlighten rather than astonish and bears in mind that the audience has come to hear the message, not to watch the messenger. He is entirely concerned with putting his idea across in a way that is clear and immediately understood. Ideally, a lecture is a monologue in form but a dialogue in essence, for the reaction of the audience, though silent, is comment of an unmistakable sort. In a transcribed lecture, the voice is there, but the accompaniment, the counterpoint provided by the audience response, is missing.

A certain amount of repetition has been unavoidable in preparing this collection. Each lecture was delivered to an audience who had never seen me before and probably would not see me again. I felt obliged to introduce my field of interest before embarking on the lecture itself, and I did so always in much the same terms. Moreover, my theme has never really varied. I have wanted people to become familiar with the contemporary American landscape and recognize its extraordinary complexity and beauty. I have reminded them that their immediate surroundings, whether urban or rural, contain a wealth of structures and spaces and compositions no less impressive than those in other parts of the world and in many instances unique to America. Over and over again I have said that the commonplace aspects of the contemporary landscape, the streets and houses and fields and places of work, could teach us a great deal not only about American history and American society but about ourselves and how we relate to the world. It is a matter of learning how to see. Several essays in this collection make that point.

I now realize that in those earlier years I put undue emphasis on the immediate visual experience of the landscape and ignored a more critical approach. But it served a useful purpose. There was a time not many years ago when the only comments we heard on the subject were the furious denunciations uttered by the environmentalists and the laments of anti-quarians to the effect that the landscape had gone downhill ever since the Civil War. It was both a duty and a pleasure to take public issue with these two archreactionary groups. Besides, our attitude toward the landscape has since then become more discriminating, and this I ascribe to a variety of influences and developments. We have become a nation of history buffs, so enamored of historical preservation that we do not know where to stop: the Appalachian log cabin, the railroad station, the Art Deco bank all seem equally deserving of the most conscientious restoring. We have almost over-night discovered the hitherto neglected virtues of popular culture: circuses, county fairs, amusement parks, skid row, the strip. In a more socially con-scious mood we worry about ecology and pollution and the exhaustion of natural resources, and clamor for the preservation of the wilderness. All these movements have the effect of making us want to see the landscape less as a phenomenon, a space or collection of spaces, than as the setting of certain human activities.

From my own point of view, that of wanting Americans to explore the landscape for its own sake, I long thought the happiest development was the discovery by the academic world of the need for accredited courses in land-scape or environmental studies. These have recently multiplied across the country and have proved to be very popular. I know little about their con-tent. I hope they are all not only informative but exciting, with many colored slides and an occasional field trip. From the few contacts I have had with students who have taken such courses I gather they have inspired many vacation trips all over the United States, and that they produce just the attitude I wish all Americans shared: an intelligent affection for the country as it is, and a vision disciplined enough to distinguish what is wrong in the landscape and should be changed from what is valuable and worthy of protection.

But the recognition of landscape studies has had other, more complicated effects. It has encouraged scholarship and research in a field that had hitherto been neglected except by cultural geographers. I am not sure that landscape studies inevitably call for the research techniques used in other disciplines. The emphasis on the use of primary sources in landscape studies would in theory at least mean that the primary source was the landscape itself, and research would entail the development of a disciplined way of looking at the physical world. But that is not what has happened. Instead, the library stacks have become the scene of action, the vicarious literary experience is sub-stituted for the experience of reality, and the product, more often than not, is an historical tidbit, impeccably researched, dealing with some remote person-age, some remote event, someone's *perception* of the landscape, of interest chiefly to other historians. Only very rarely is there a glimpse of the history of the landscape itself, how it was formed, how it has changed, and who it was who changed it, and even more rarely does landscape research produce any speculation about the *nature* of the American landscape. I am sorry to say, much of this laborious work seems to me to be little more than local history with a spatial dimension thrown in for good measure. If the academic com-munity thinks this is an important contribution, this is where I depart from the academic community.

I admit that I am prejudiced against the current American enthusiasm for historic preservation on the small-town, middle-class scale. I admit that I hold the peculiar belief that the value of history is what it teaches us about the future. But I think that I am on firm ground when I say that most of this landscape history deals with an infinitely small fraction of the landscape—whether of the eighteenth or nineteenth century. The reason for this is sim-ple: the origin and history of only a very few spaces, very few structures are on record. Those for which we have plans and maps and legal documenta-tion and official descriptions are being studied and written about. But an infinitely greater number of structures and spaces have no documentation at all. That is why landscape history as now conceived dwells almost exclusively on such public documented spaces as the national parks, New England colo-nial villages, Savannah and Williamsburg, a handful of gardens and monu-ments and battlefields, and on the already restored towns and buildings, and has nothing to say about the rest of the landscape. The same limitations prevail in architectural history and for the same reason: lack of documenta-tion. It may be objected that this is a very good reason. I am inclined to disagree. I believe that with the use of modern archeological techniques, with the use of aerial photography, above all with the use of more imagination, more speculation we could immensely expand our knowledge of the land-scape of the past.

In the meantime we should at least recognize that there is another aspect of the landscape, contemporary as well as historical, that we know little about: for those documented spaces—political spaces in the sense that most of them were created by some formal legislative act—are and always have been sur-rounded by other spaces of a humbler, less permanent, less conspicuous sort. One of the rewards of having to edit these essays has been the discovery that over the course of years I have gradually become aware of that other land-scape element. At first all that mattered was well-defined, permanent, "estab-lished" village or town or landscape, self-sufficient, well adjusted, and happily conscious of its unique quality.

But gradually, out of the corner of my eye, so to speak, I saw a disturbing mobility of people and spaces, a search for adjustment, for change; an incessant making of structures and spaces and communities, an incessant adaptation and remaking of the landscape, resisted by the political landscape when it could no longer be ignored. In the last essay in this collection—and the last one to be written—I have tried to redefine my idea of landscape to include this fluid ingredient, and I have dutifully recommended a balance between the forces of stability and those of mobility as a way to achieve the best landscape for the future. But it is not the role of the landscape student to make recommendations. If he has any role at all it is to teach people to learn by seeing. I would be more than content if I could myself learn to distinguish between these two very different but complementary elements in our landscape: one established and maintained and governed by law and political institutions, dedicated to permanence and planned evolution; the other, the vernacular landscape, identified with local custom, pragmatic adaptation to circumstances, and unpredictable mobility. All that I can now undertake is a tentative investigation of one element in that second landscape: the vernacular dwelling. Even so, I suspect that it is by studying the vernacular that we will eventually reach a comprehensive definition of landscape and of landscape beauty. The older I grow and the longer I look at landscapes and seek to understand them, the more convinced I am that their beauty is not simply an aspect but their very essence and that that beauty derives from the human presence. For far too long we have told ourselves that the beauty of a landscape was the expression of some transcendent law: the conformity to certain universal esthetic principles or the conformity to certain biological or ecological laws. But this is true only of formal or planned political landscapes. The beauty that we see in the vernacular landscape is the image of our common humanity: hard work, stubborn hope, and mutual forbearance striving to be love. I believe that a landscape which makes these qualities manifest is one that can be called beautiful.

J.B.J.

The innovators whom I oppose are turning off attention from life to nature. They seem to think that we are placed here to watch the growth of plants, or the motions of the stars. Socrates was rather of the opinion, that what we had to learn was, how to do good, and avoid evil.

—Samuel Johnson, *John Milton*

The Word Itself

Rio Grande Valley north of Santa Fe. Seen from the air, the difference between the two landscapes is most marked. (Photo: Laura Gilpin)

Why is it, I wonder, that we have trouble agreeing on the meaning of *landscape?* The word is simple enough, and it refers to something which we think we understand; and yet to each of us it seems to mean something different.

What we need is a new definition. The one we find in most dictionaries is more than three hundred years old and was drawn up for artists. It tells us that a landscape is a "portion of land which the eye can comprehend at a glance." Actually when it was first introduced (or reintroduced) into English it did not mean the view itself, it meant a *picture* of it, an artist's interpretation. It was his task to take the forms and colors and spaces in front of him— mountains, river, forest, fields, and so on—and compose them so that they made a work of art.

There is no need to tell in detail how the word gradually changed in meaning. First it meant a picture of a view; then the view itself. We went into the country and discovered beautiful views, always remembering the criteria of landscape beauty as established by critics and artists. Finally, on a modest scale, we undertook to make over a piece of ground so that it resembled a pastoral landscape in the shape of a garden or park. Just as the painter used his judgment as to what to include or omit in his composition, the landscape gardener (as he was known in the eighteenth century) took pains to produce a stylized "picturesque" landscape, leaving out the muddy roads, the plowed fields, the squalid villages of the real countryside and including certain agreeable natural features: brooks and groves of trees and smooth expanses of grass. The results were often extremely beautiful, but they were still pictures, though in three dimensions.

The reliance on the artist's point of view and his definition of landscape beauty persisted throughout the nineteenth century. Olmsted and his followers designed their parks and gardens in "painterly" terms. "Although three-dimensional composition in landscape materials differs from two-dimensional landscape painting, because a garden or park design contains a *series* of pictorial compositions," the *Encyclopaedia Britannica* (13th edition) informs us, ". . . nevertheless in each of these pictures we find the familiar basic principles of unity, of repetition, of sequence and balance, of harmony and contrast." But within the last half century a revolution has taken place: landscape design and landscape painting have gone their separate ways. Landscape architects no longer turn to Poussin or Salvator Rosa or Gilpin for inspiration; they may not even have heard of their work. Knowledge of ecology and conservation and environmental psychology are now part of the landscape architect's professional background, and protecting and "managing" the natural environment are seen as more important than the designing of picturesque parks. Environmental designers, I have noticed, avoid the word *landscape* and prefer *land* or *terrain* or *environment* or even *space* when

3

they have a specific site in mind. *Landscape* is used for suggesting the esthetic quality of the wider countryside.

As for painters, they have long since lost interest in producing conventional landscapes. Kenneth Clark, in his book *Landscape into Painting*, comments on this fact. "The microscope and telescope have so greatly enlarged the range of our vision," he writes, "that the snug, sensible nature which we can see with our own eyes has ceased to satisfy our imaginations. We know that by our new standards of measurement the most extensive landscape is practically the same as the hole through which the burrowing ant escapes from our sight."[1]

This does not strike me as a very satisfactory explanation of the demise of traditional landscape painting. More than a change in scale was responsible. Painters have learned to see the environment in a new and more subjective manner: as a different kind of experience. But that is not the point. The point is, the two disciplines which once had a monopoly on the word—landscape architecture and landscape painting—have ceased to use it the way they did a few decades ago, and it has now reverted as it were to the public domain.

What has happened to the word in the meantime? For one thing we are using it with much more freedom. We no longer bother with its literal meaning—which I will come to later—and we have coined a number of words similar to it: roadscape, townscape, cityscape, as if the syllable *scape* meant a space, which it does not; and we speak of the wilderness landscape, the lunar landscape, even of the landscape at the bottom of the ocean. Furthermore the word is frequently used in critical writing as a kind of metaphor. Thus we find mention of the "landscape of a poet's images," "the landscape of dreams," or "landscape as antagonist" or "the landscape of thought," or, on quite a different level, the "political landscape of the NATO conference," the "patronage landscape." Our first reaction to these usages is that they are farfetched and pretentious. Yet they remind us of an important truth: that we always need a word or phrase to indicate a kind of environment or setting which can give vividness to a thought or event or relationship; a background placing it in the world. In this sense *landscape* serves the same useful purpose as do the words *climate* or *atmosphere,* used metaphorically. In fact *landscape* when used as a painter's term often meant "all that part of a picture which is not of the body or argument"—like the stormy array of clouds in a battle scene or the glimpse of the Capitol in a presidential portrait. In the eighteenth century, *landscape* indicated scenery in the theater and had the function of discreetly suggesting the location of the action or perhaps the time of day. As I have suggested elsewhere, there is no better indication of how our relation to the environment can change over the centuries than in the role of stage scenery. Three hundred years ago Corneille could write a five-act tragedy with a single indication of the setting: "The action takes place in the palace of the king." If we glance at the work of a modern playwright we will probably find one detailed description of a scene after another, and the ultimate in this kind of landscape, I suppose, is the contemporary movie. Here the set does much more than merely identify the time and place and establish the mood. By means of shifts in lighting and sound and perspective the set actually creates the players, identifies them, and tells them what to do: a good example of environmental determinism.

But these scenic devices and theater landscapes are mere imitations of real ones: easily understood by almost everyone, and shared. What I object to is the fallacy in the metaphorical use of the word. No one denies that as our thoughts become complex and abstract we need metaphors to give them a degree of reality. No one denies that as we become uncertain of our status we need more and more reenforcement from our environment. But we should not use the word *landscape* to describe our private world, our private micro-cosm, and for a simple reason: a landscape is a concrete, three-dimensional shared reality.

Lands and Shapes

Landscape is a space on the surface of the earth; intuitively we know that it is a space with a degree of permanence, with its own distinct character, either topographical or cultural, and above all a space shared by a group of people; and when we go beyond the dictionary definition of landscape and examine the word itself we find that our intuition is correct.

Landscape is a compound, and its components hark back to that ancient Indo-European idiom, brought out of Asia by migrating peoples thousands of years ago, that became the basis of almost all modern European languages—Latin and Celtic and Germanic and Slavic and Greek. The word was introduced into Britain sometime after the fifth century A.D. by the Angles and Saxons and Jutes and Danes and other groups of Germanic speech. In addition to its Old English variations—*landskipe, landscaef,* and others—there is the German *landschaft,* the Dutch *landscap,* as well as Danish and Swedish equivalents. They all come from the same roots, but they are not always used in the English sense. A German *landschaft,* for instance, can sometimes be a small administrative unit, corresponding in size to our ward. I have the feeling that there is evolving a slight but noticeable difference between the way we Americans use the word and the way the English do. We tend to think that *landscape* can mean natural scenery only, whereas in England a landscape almost always contains a human element.

The equivalent word in Latin languages derives in almost every case from the Latin *pagus*—meaning a defined rural district. The French, in fact, have several words for *landscape,* each with shades of meaning: *terroir, pays, paysage, campagne*. In England the distinction was once made between two kinds of landscape: woodland and champion—the latter deriving from the French *champagne,* meaning a countryside of fields.

That first syllable, *land,* has had a varied career. By the time it reached England it signified *earth* and *soil* as well as a portion of the surface of the globe. But a much earlier Gothic meaning was *plowed field*. Grimm's monumental dictionary of the German language says that "*land* originally signified the plot of ground or the furrows in a field that were annually rotated" or redistributed. We can assume that in the Dark Ages the most common use of the word indicated any well-defined portion of the earth's surface. A small farm plot was a land, and so was a sovereign territory like England or Scotland; any area with recognized boundaries was a land. Despite almost two thousand years of reinterpretation by geographers and poets and ecologists, *land* in American law remains stubbornly true to that ancient meaning: "any *definite* site regarded as a portion of the earth's surface, and extending in both vertical directions as defined by law" (italics added).

Perhaps because of this definition farmers think of land not only in terms of soil and topography but in terms of spatial measurements, as a defined portion of a wider area. In the American South, and in England too, a "land" is a subdivision of a field, a broad row made by plowing or mowing, and horse-drawn mowers were once advertised as "making a land of so-and-so many feet." In Yorkshire the reapers of wheat take a "land" (generally six feet wide) and go down the length of the field. "A woman," says the *English Dialect Dictionary,* "would thus reap half an acre a day and a man an acre." In his book on English field systems, Gray mentions a typical medieval village where the two large, open fields "consisted of about two thousand long narrow 'lands' or selions [furrows] each containing usually from one fourth of an acre to an acre."[2]

This is very confusing, and even more confusing is the fact that to this day in Scotland a *land* means a building divided into houses or flats. I confess that I find this particular use of the word hard to decipher, except that in Gaelic the word *lann* means an enclosed space. Finally, here is an example—if it can be called that—of *land* meaning both a fraction of a larger space and an enclosed space: infantrymen know that a land is an interval between the grooves of a rifle bore.

I need not press the point. As far back as we can trace the word, *land* meant a defined space, one with boundaries, though not necessarily one with fences or walls. The word has so many derivative meanings that it rivals in ambiguity the word *landscape*. Three centuries ago it was still being used in everyday speech to signify a fraction of plowed ground no larger than a quarter acre, then to signify an expanse of village holdings, as in grassland or woodland, and then finally to signify England itself—the largest space any Englishman of those days could imagine; in short, a remarkably versatile word, but always implying a space defined by people, and one that could be described in legal terms.

This brings us to that second syllable: *scape*. It is essentially the same as *shape*, except that it once meant a composition of *similar* objects, as when we speak of a fellowship or a membership. The meaning is clearer in a related word: *sheaf*—a bundle or collection of similar stalks or plants. Old English, or Anglo-Saxon, seems to have contained several compound words using the second syllable—*scape* or its equivalent—to indicate collective aspects of the environment. It is much as if the words had been coined when people began to see the complexities of the man-made world. Thus *housescape* meant what we would now call a household, and a word of the same sort which we still use—*township*—once meant a collection of "tuns" or farmsteads.

Taken apart in this manner, *landscape* appears to be an easily understood word: a collection of lands. But both syllables once had several distinct, now forgotten meanings, and this should alert us to the fact that familiar mono-syllables in English—house, town, land, field, home—can be very shifty de-spite their countrified sound. *Scape* is an instance. An English document of the tenth century mentions the destruction of what it called a "waterscape." What could that have been? We might logically suppose that it was the liquid equivalent of a landscape, an ornamental arrangement, perhaps, of ponds and brooks and waterfalls, the creation of some Anglo-Saxon predecessor of Olmsted's. But it was actually something entirely different. The waterscape in question was a system of pipes and drains and aqueducts serving a residence and a mill.

From this piece of information we can learn two things. First, that our Dark Age forebears possessed skills which we probably did not credit them with, and second, that the word *scape* could also indicate something like an organization or a system. And why not? If *housescape* meant the organization of the personnel of a house, if *township* eventually came to mean an admin-istrative unit, then *landscape* could well have meant something like an organi-zation, a system of rural farm spaces. At all events it is clear that a thousand years ago the word had nothing to do with scenery or the depiction of scenery.

We pull up the word *landscape* by its Indo-European roots in an attempt to gain some insight into its basic meaning, and at first glance the results seem disappointing. Aside from the fact that as originally used the word dealt only with a small fraction of the rural environment, it seems to contain not a hint of the esthetic and emotional associations which the word still has for us. Little is to be gained by searching for some etymological link between our own rich landscape and the small cluster of plowed fields of more than a thousand years ago.

Nevertheless the formula *landscape as a composition of man-made spaces on the land* is more significant than it first appears, for if it does not provide us with a definition it throws a revealing light on the origin of the concept. For it says that a landscape is not a natural feature of the environment but a *synthetic* space, a man-made system of spaces superimposed on the face of the land, functioning and evolving not according to natural laws but to serve a community—for the collective character of the landscape is one thing that all generations and all points of view have agreed upon. A landscape is thus a space deliberately created to speed up or slow down the process of nature. As Eliade expresses it, it represents man taking upon himself the role of time.

A very successful undertaking on the whole, and the proof, paradoxically enough, is that many if not most of these synthetic organizations of space have been so well assimilated into the natural environment that they are indistinguishable and unrecognized for what they are. The reclamation of Holland, of the Fens, of large portions of the Po Valley are familiar examples of a topographical intervention producing new landscapes. Less well known are the synthetic landscapes produced simply by spatial reorganization. Historians are said to be blind to the spatial dimension of history, which is probably why we hear so little about the wholesale making of agricultural landscapes throughout seventeenth-century Europe.

It is not a coincidence that much of this landscape creation took place during a period when the greatest gardens and parks and the most magnificent of city complexes were being designed. A narrow and pedantic taxonomy has persuaded us that there is little or nothing in common between what used to be called civil engineering and garden or landscape architecture, but in fact from an historical perspective their more successful accomplishments are identical in result. The two professions may work for different patrons, but they both reorganize space for human needs, both produce works of art in the truest sense of the term. In the contemporary world it is by recognizing this similarity of purpose that we will eventually formulate a new definition of *landscape:* a composition of man-made or man-modified spaces to serve as infrastructure or background for our collective existence; and if *background* seems inappropriately modest we should remember that in our modern use of the word it means that which underscores not only our identity and presence, but also our history.

It is not for me to attempt to elaborate on this new definition. My contribution would in any event be peripheral, for my interest in the topic is confined to trying to see how certain organizations of space can be identified with certain social and religious attitudes, especially here in America. This is not a new approach, for it has long been common among architectural and landscape architectural historians; and it leaves many important aspects of the contemporary landscape and contemporary city entirely unexplored. But it has the virtue of including the visual experience of our everyday world and of allowing me to remain loyal to that old-fashioned but surprisingly persistent definition of *landscape:* "A portion of the earth's surface that can be comprehended at a glance."

A Pair of Ideal Landscapes

Connecticut interstate highway, Norwalk. (Connecticut State Highway Department)

◄ *Pecan groves and small truck farms near Little Rock, Arkansas. (Leonard Photographic Services)*

Those of us who undertake to study landscapes in a serious way soon come up against a sobering truth: even the simplest, least interesting landscape often contains elements which we are quite unable to explain, mysteries that fit into no known pattern. But we also eventually learn that every landscape, no matter how exotic, also contains elements which we at once recognize and understand. We may be baffled by the layout of the towns and the crops the people raise, and the architecture may be unlike anything we have encountered, but the fields and fences and houses, for instance, are easy to understand; we have only to look at them once to see the role they play.

It is with such commonplace elements that we should begin our study. The unique features can be taken care of later. The familiar serves as a point of departure; it reassures us that however strange the landscape may appear to be, it is not entirely alien and is related to every other landscape. Human nature satisfies its needs in many ways, but the needs are everywhere essentially the same.

Human nature is a risky topic to discuss, and not a few persons will maintain that no such thing exists. Yet there are some assumptions about the universality of human behavior that are so obvious that we accept them without question. One of them is that none of us, no matter how self-reliant we may be, can survive alone for any extended length of time. How long that time can be is something we really do not know, and I daresay it is one of the things about human nature that we have yet to learn. Nevertheless there is a limit. There comes a moment when we begin to suffer, psychologically and even physically, for the companionship and presence of others. Ethologists and others who study animal behavior and know much about the gregarious or social characteristics of birds and animals and fish and even of insects, tell how they respond to the presence of others of their kind and seem to languish when they are alone too long. So we are not unique in this respect; but we are much more demanding. The mere presence of other bodies is not enough. We have the need for sustained discourse, for the exchange of ideas and, what is no less essential, for disagreement, since both kinds of communication lead to a sharpened sense of our identity. That is why gregariousness never suffices; that is why we are not content until our social instincts are given form and even a kind of visibility. We are what Aristotle called political animals;. animals, that is to say, having the power of speech, which enables us to debate such matters as good and evil, justice and injustice, and how to act to achieve a good life.

Yes. But what complicates our identity is the fact that we are also inhabitants of the earth, involved in the natural order and in a sense even part of it. This means that we have to spend time and thought and energy on providing ourselves with shelter and food and clothing and a degree of security. We have to come to terms with nature if we are to survive. We have to understand nature and feel at home with it if we are to be true inhabitants of the earth.

11

It is a romantic error to suppose that this experience should be solitary. If we hunt, if we farm, even if we botanize, we are benefiting from and sharing in the accumulated experience of others, so this other identity of ours also has its social implications. It implies that we recognize other people as inhabitants of the earth as well as members of a social order. It is the interaction of these two very different and sometimes contradictory definitions of man that produces a landscape—an environment modified by the permanent presence of a group. No group sets out to create a landscape, of course. What it sets out to do is to create a community, and the landscape as its visible manifestation is simply the by-product of people working and living, sometimes coming together, sometimes staying apart, but always recognizing their interdependence.

There is invariably tension between the two points of view, the two identities, always debate as to which is the more important, and we do well to recognize that this tension is not confined to the group; it is also within each of us. None of us is ever entirely political animal or entirely inhabitant; we are unpredictable mixtures of the two. We enjoy the dense vitality of the city only to complain that there are not enough green spaces where we can be alone with nature. To live close to nature in the open country is a wholesome experience—if only there were more political coming together!

It follows that no landscape can be exclusively devoted to the fostering of only one identity. Our imaginative literature abounds in descriptions of utopias where everyone is civic-minded, and there are many descriptions of the delights of living in harmony with nature as certain pretechnological societies presumably did. But we sense that these visions are not true to human nature as we know it, and that these landscapes can never be realized; and that is why many of us find utopian speculations unprofitable.

Still, we cannot expect any landscape to be a perfect blend of the two points of view. One of them is always favored over the other, and an interesting aspect of landscape history is how the two can alternate. This process is well illustrated in our own American landscape history, and it is in order to understand that history that I am enumerating some of the simplest and most visible elements in what can be called the political landscape: the landscape which evolved partly out of experience, partly from design, to meet some of the needs of men and women in their political guise. The political elements I have in mind are such things as walls and boundaries and highways and monuments and public places; these have a definite role to play in the landscape. They exist to insure order and security and continuity and to give citizens a visible status. They serve to remind us of our rights and obligations and of our history.

Elements such as these are what every society is likely to value, and every landscape, whatever its complexion, will contain *some* of them. Nevertheless there are certain historical landscapes where they are especially numerous.

Fifth-century Greece is the best-known example of a political landscape. The writings of Plato and Aristotle, the legislation of Solon and Cleisthenes provide us with the earliest descriptions of such a landscape and how it was brought into being. Republican Rome also had its political landscape and so did seventeenth-century France, and one of the most extensive as well as one of the most familiar examples is our own American landscape as first laid out in the early nineteenth century. Many more could be cited: ancient China and ancient Japan produced impressive political landscapes, and the Communist countries are doubtless producing them now. On the other hand, the landscapes of medieval Europe and of many Moslem countries seem to have contained comparatively few political elements, and I think it could be said that in the contemporary United States they are less conspicuous than they were a century and a half ago.

That, however, is something we can ascertain only by studying the political landscape of the past in greater detail.

Boundaries

The most basic political element in any landscape is the boundary. Politically speaking what matters first is the formation of a community of responsible citizens, a well-defined territory composed of small holdings and a number of public spaces; so the first step toward organizing space is the defining of that territory, after which we divide it for the individual members. Boundaries, therefore, unmistakable, permanent, inviolate boundaries, are essential.

We would all agree that insofar as every landscape is a composition of spaces it is also a composition or web of boundaries. But here we must be cautious, for boundaries can serve a variety of functions. In the contemporary Western world we assume that a boundary is the point (or line) of contact between two defined spaces, a way of regulating contact and communication with neighbors, even while it protects us against invasion or unwanted entry. We assume—and rightly from our point of view—that the boundary is like a skin: a thin surface which is in fact part of the body, part of space which it protects. We therefore assume that the boundary corresponds as closely as possible to the area of the content. That is why we have spent so much time and thought establishing natural or functional boundaries for every kind of space, boundaries which faithfully delimit a homogeneous unit. In geographical terms we try to discover a forest or a range of hills which will divide one area or region from another, or to locate the line marking a difference in language or religion or ethnic stock. Planners and sociologists are no less concerned with establishing the boundaries of economic or social territories, and so we have boundaries based on the circulation of newspapers or the drawing capacity of a shopping center. In every case we try to establish a boundary closely adjusted to its social or natural content, and back of this effort is the notion that the space (or the way the space is used) is an essential characteristic of the contents. A nation, we say, is not simply a collection of people, it is also the territory they occupy, and the boundary in consequence should be drawn so that the two entities correspond as closely as possible.

This may seem obvious, but there is reason to believe that the traditional political landscape had a very different concept of a boundary: it was intended less to define a region and establish an effective relationship with the outside world than to isolate and protect something within it. It was not so much a skin as it was a packaging, an envelope.

Therefore the boundary in a political landscape often bears little relationship to the society within it, and a good illustration of this can be seen in the United States. In the nineteenth century we created a number of states which were in effect immense rectangular spaces having no relation to topography or population. In the beginning a few thousand settlers constituted the entire population of an area the size of a European kingdom.

In those politically minded times, no one protested the incongruity. What mattered was that a territory was established in which certain political institutions could begin to function without outside interference.

A typical man-made space in a political landscape, whether farm or village or nation, is likely to contain near its center an isolated, independent structure surrounded by a buffer zone and a very visible boundary, and communication between this structure (or collection of structures) and the outside world is formalized in some manner: by a portal or gate or architectural entrance way. As we might expect, this kind of protective, isolating boundary was common in ancient Greece.

In his book on the Classical city, Fustel de Coulanges describes how the center of the farmstead, the sacred hearth, was surrounded by such a buffer zone. "The sacred fire must be isolated—that is to say, completely separated from all that is not itself. . . . There must be an enclosure around this hearth at a certain distance." At a later period when dwellings were of necessity brought closer together in towns and cities, the sacred enclosure persisted in the form of a low wall, a ditch, or even a mere open space a few feet wide. "At Rome the law fixed two feet and a half as the width of the open space, which was always to separate two houses, and this space was consecrated to the 'god of the enclosure.'"[1]

Even the city states of Classical Greece possessed boundaries meant to isolate and protect, and when possible to *prevent* contact. Topographical features—mountains or rivers—rarely served as barriers, but it was generally agreed that each territory or landscape should be isolated. Thucydides tells how "Athens accused the Megarians of pushing their cultivation into the consecrated and unenclosed land on the border" between the two; and that violation triggered the Peloponnesian war.[2]

The Roman *Limes* was not an international boundary in the modern sense.

It was a long, continuous, fortified zone of some width that represented not a division between two military powers but simply the outermost limits of Roman influence; it was the *rejection* of contact. "This unduly praised frontier," says Toynbee, "really registered nothing but the undesigned and accidental locus of the geographical line along which two conflicting social forces had come into a transitory equilibrium."[3]

In a greatly modified form, our early American landscape displayed much the same attitude toward boundaries: they were designed to isolate and protect the objects or people within them. The device persisted longest, I think, in the siting of important buildings: the freestanding church, the freestanding courthouse, the freestanding school or college building—all of them edifices of some sanctity—relied on an enclosing-and-excluding-fence or wall and a surrounding buffer zone of empty space to give them dignity and aloofness. We are grateful that they did, for the result was almost always a composition of great effectiveness. But it is *we* who have learned to perceive that composition; the classical building of white clapboard or brick in the midst of smooth, green lawn and towering trees, fenced off from the secular world is in our eyes a single harmonious unit. Yet I cannot help feel that when those structures were built they were in no way seen as related to the open space encompassing them. That space was merely the protective envelope or packaging, and the fence or wall was merely the ultimate legal symbol of autonomy.

We have outgrown this protective or exclusionary concept of the boundary, and generally speaking the linear boundary, duly surveyed, registered, and indicated on the landscape is the one we prefer. We are all familiar with Frost's poem "Mending Wall," in which a farmer insists on mending the wall between his property and that of his neighbor, even though neither landowner has any livestock. "Good fences make good neighbors," he keeps saying. Frost comments: "He moves in darkness as it seems to me, / Not of woods only and the shade of trees. / He will not go behind his father's saying, / And he likes having thought of it so well / He says again, 'Good fences make good neighbors.'"

He is right to this extent: boundaries stabilize social relationships. They make residents out of the homeless, neighbors out of strangers, strangers out of enemies. They give a permanent human quality to what would otherwise be an amorphous stretch of land. Those roughly geometrical enclosed spaces are a way of rebuking the disorder and shapelessness of the natural environment; seeing them from outside, the alien wanderer wishes he too belonged. It is when we find ourselves in a landscape of well-built, well-maintained fences and hedges and walls, whether in New England or Europe or Mexico, that we realize we are in a landscape where political identity is a matter of importance, a landscape where lawyers make a good living and everyone knows how much land he owns.

But the reliance on the linear boundary is relatively new. Not until the very end of the eighteenth century was the first linear national boundary—that of France—officially established and inscribed on maps; at much the same time that in America we were designing whole landscapes with accurately defined linear boundaries when we passed the Northwest Ordinance in 1787. Boundaries, especially boundaries sanctified by law, are hard to obliterate, and our national grid system, the triumph of geometry over topography, will be with us till the end of time. Nevertheless there are signs that we are growing tired of linear boundaries—at least we are growing tired of *seeing* them. On an individual scale we are beginning to suspect that walls and fences are a costly nuisance to build and maintain, occupy much space, and far from guaranteeing privacy, actually invite vandalism and intrusion. Even national boundaries are becoming more flexible, and when public opinion disapproves on moral or esthetic or economic grounds of boundaries and frontiers we can be fairly certain that the political role of the landscape is no longer paramount and that we have begun interpreting it in other terms.

So boundaries which are highly visible and jealously protected, boundaries whether linear or of that buffer variety, belong in landscapes designed by—and for—political animals, and often for four-footed animals as well.

Forum Follows Function

When we hear mention of political spaces and their value, what comes to mind is the familiar space—plaza or market or town square or forum—where we gather to enjoy the company of others and pass the time of day. It would be hard to find a community without such a space: alive and full of action, with people buying and selling, talking and listening, walking and looking about, or merely resting. Sometimes the space is the civic center, ornate and immense, sometimes it is nothing more than an empty lot or a wide space in the street. It is always enjoyable, and instinct tells us that a public space of one kind or another is essential to any community.

But there is a great variety in the way these public spaces are used, and a great variety in the groups of people who use them. In a political landscape they play a very different role than they do in a landscape like that of contemporary America. Architectural and urban historians often analyze them as works of art, and indeed that is what many of them seem to be, but it is their social function that we should look at first of all. In his book *Town and Square* Paul Zucker defines the space as one "which makes a community a community and not merely an aggregate of individuals . . . a gathering place for the people, humanizing them by mutual contact, providing them with a shelter against the haphazard traffic, and freeing them from the tension of rushing through a web of streets."

Here is a characteristically modern definition of the public square: a place of passive enjoyment, a kind of playground for adults, and it says a good deal about how slack our current definition of community can be. Zucker and many others are content to describe the public square strictly in terms of gregariousness: how it offers a spatial experience shared by a heterogeneous public which will sooner or later go its separate ways; an urban form which acts to draw people together and give them a momentary pleasure and sense of well-being. No one should underestimate those benefits, but in the political landscape the public square serves an entirely different purpose. It is assumed that those who come there are *already* aware that they are members of the community, responsible citizens, and that on occasion they will participate in public discussions and take action on behalf of the community.

True, every traditional public square has served several ends: marketplace, a place of business and a place of informal sociability and amusement, a place for pageantry. The agora in Athens, far from being architecturally impressive, was a jumble of crowded downtown streets and irregular open spaces where shrines and altars, public buildings and monuments stood in the midst of workshops, market stalls, and taverns. For Athenians of conservative tastes, as R. E. Wycherley reminds us, "the agora was the haunt of the dregs of the populace, the home of idleness, vulgarity and gossip."[4] Aristotle, who thought of the agora chiefly as a place for discussion and the exchange of ideas, described in *The Politics* his ideal public square: All commercial activities and all merchants and vendors were to be exiled to another part of town. "Nothing here [in the agora] may be bought or sold, and no member of the lower order may be admitted unless summoned by the authorities. . . . The market proper, where buying and selling are done, must be in quite a separate place, conveniently situated both for goods sent up from the harbor and for people coming in from the country."[5]

Aristotle's suggestions were ignored in antiquity, but they seem to have inspired some of the features of the Spanish colonial towns laid out according to the Laws of the Indies. Their produce market was located outside the plaza, and the presence of Indians was strictly controlled.

To see one of these traditional public squares in action, or better yet to take part in the action, is one of the greatest pleasures the tourist can know. Nothing is more festive than the corso in a Mexican plaza after dark, with the band playing, the women strolling clockwise around the square while the men go counterclockwise. And what is more colorful than a Moslem market or bazaar? No wonder every American wishes we had more such places in our cities. An eminent architect has gone so far as to say that the plaza is the basis of civilization and that our failure to have examples is a sign of American decadence. But there are those who have grown weary of our cult of the plaza as the solution to all our urban problems. Robert Venturi holds that "architects have been bewitched by a single element in the Italian landscape: the piazza. . . . [They] have been brought up on Space, and enclosed space is the easiest to handle."[6]

I am inclined to agree, though my objection to the contemporary American plaza derives from a suspicion that most of its proponents do not really understand what it is. They think of it as an environment, a stage set, yet it has always been something much more worthwhile than that. It was, and in many places still is, a manifestation of the local social order, of the relationship between citizens and between citizens and the authority of the state. The plaza is where the role of the individual in the community is made visible, where we reveal our identity as part of an ethnic or religious or political or consumer-oriented society, and it exists and functions to reinforce that identity.

That is one reason for learning to perceive the urban public space not simply in esthetic or environmental terms, but in terms of history. When we do that we discover that there are many different kinds of squares, each with its own ideology, its own origin often at odds with its everyday appearance. Urbanists and architects, in keeping with that fascination with Space that Venturi decries, praise the immense, open, unencumbered space or plaza of the Pueblo villages of the Southwest as the perfect center for the fostering of community interaction. But the fact of the matter is, the Pueblo plaza is primarily the site of periodic religious ceremonies, and its focal point is a shrine called the World Navel, the place of communication with the ancestral spirits. Casual sociability—at least until recently—was confined to the flat roofs of the surrounding houses.

Every traditional public space, whether religious or political or ethnic in character, displays a variety of symbols, inscriptions, images, monuments, not as works of art but to remind people of their civic privileges and duties— and tacitly to exclude the outsider. The Roman Forum was cluttered with such reminders, and though the colonial New England town was hostile to public art it nevertheless contained a number of powerful symbols, impossible to misinterpret: the church with its steeple and bell, its front door covered with public notices and decrees; the whipping post, the stocks, the graveyard, and sometimes the tree ceremoniously planted by the first settlers. All of these served to tell those who came to the church services or town meeting or to the militia drill that they were part of a tight-knit religious community and had obligations. The public space was not for relaxation or environmental awareness; it was for *civic* awareness.

As we might expect, the ideal public square in the political landscape has a strong architectural quality. It occupies the most prestigious location in the principal town and is surrounded by politically significant buildings: law court, archives, treasury, legislative hall, and often military headquarters and jail as well. The space itself is adorned with statues of local heroes and divinities, monuments to important historic events. All important ceremonies are enacted here. Typical of the political emphasis on boundaries, the area is well defined by markers and has its own laws and its own officers. Finally, it is here in the agora or forum that history is made visible and where speech becomes a political instrument, eloquence a form of political action.

What is the origin of this space dedicated to public debate and public visibility? Jean-Pierre Vernant in his studies of historical psychology traces the evolution of the agora from the practice of the special warrior class of ancient Greece of periodically assembling in military formation—in a circle, that is to say—to discuss matters of common concern. One after another, the men step into the circle and freely express themselves. When each has finished, he steps back and another takes his place and says his piece. The circle is thus a place of free speech and debate. In the course of time this agora (the word means "assembly") becomes the meeting of all qualified citizens; they too debate matters of common interest. Vernant comments: "[T]he human group creates this image of itself: along with the private dwellings there is a center where public affairs are discussed, and this center represents everything that is 'common,' the collectivity as such. In this center all persons are on a footing of equality, no one is inferior to anyone else. . . . We here see the birth of a society in which the relationships between man and man are perceived as identical, symmetrical, interchangeable. . . . It could be said that by having access to this circular space known as the agora, citizens become part of a political system based on balance, symmetry, reciprocity."[7]

Vernant goes on to speculate on how this notion of equality and interchangeability may well have inspired Hippodamus to create the grid city plan of identical, interchangeable blocks.

In seventeenth-century France something resembling a new political landscape emerged, and there, in consequence, the public square became a work of art—a place where the social hierarchy could display itself to best advantage. We Americans later produced our own version—less elaborate, no doubt, but more faithful to the classic prototype. For more than half a century after the Revolution we remained loyal to the national political landscape of identical, interchangeable townships all centered on the county seat with its courthouse square. I have suggested elsewhere how that tradition lingered longer in the South than in other regions. The memory of the classical public space as the place of oratory and as the safeguard of democracy died hard, and no longer than seventy-five years ago we undertook to bring it back to life—statues, colonnades, and fountain—in the grandiose form known as the City Beautiful. Civic centers in San Francisco, Denver, Washington, and other cities still testify to its brief popularity.

I think we have finally come to recognize that we no longer know how to use the traditional public space as an effective political instrument, and that we need a wide choice of very different kinds of public space. No one has written more perceptively on the matter than William H. Whyte. In a recent article telling of his extensive research into how such spaces are used in New York, he makes it plain that what we now want most of all is an agreeable "environmental" experience.[8] The most popular, most frequented plazas and small parks are those which (he says) provide an agreeable microclimate, easy accessibility, some sensational object like a piece of sculpture or a display of flowing water, and which (this is most essential) allow people to sit comfortably and relax. "What attracts people most," he concludes, ". . . are other people." But what does other people mean? Those with whom (to use Aristotle's phrase) we can exchange "moral or noble ideas"? No; "other people" more often than not in this new urban space seems to mean voices and color and movement and fleeting impressions. People have become elements of animation in a pleasantly planned environment, and we are social beings merely to the extent that we want to be "at one" with that particular environment.

These contemporary urban parks, I cannot help feeling, are the last poor remnants of what was once an almost sacred space, but in our rejection of their political function we presage not the end of civilization but the end of one chapter. We are better off than we suppose; our landscape has an undreamed of potential for public spaces of infinite variety. When we look back a century, or even a half century, we realize how many new public or common spaces have appeared in our towns and cities, spaces where people come together spontaneously and without restraint. I am thinking of how the role of the college campus has changed, even in my own day. A half century ago it was a jealously guarded academic grove, surrounded by a fence and looked upon by the public with a mixture of envy and contempt. It now plays a leading role in the cultural life of all classes in the community. In the high school auditorium many smaller communities not only come in contact with ideas but discuss them in meetings. The sports arena belongs in a different class, but in one respect it is the legitimate successor of the agora or forum: it is where we demonstrate local loyalties—loudly as the Greeks would have done and with gestures. The flea market is a new and unpredictable public space and so is the strip. If their humanizing function seems doubtful that may be because they have yet to develop, but even now there can be no doubt as to their popularity.

It is next to impossible to enumerate all the new spaces we are using and enjoying together. Wherever we look we see a new one: the cluster of campers in a recreation area, the Sunday meetings of classic car buffs in the empty parking lots of supermarkets, outdoor revivals, protest parades, stamp collectors' markets, family reunions, and the picnics of the sons and daughters of Iowa—all of them public, all of them fulfilling in one manner or another the needs once met in a single, consecrated space.

In the meantime the obsolete courthouse is demolished and replaced by a parking garage, and a giant Calder mobile takes the place of the statue to a Civil War general, and downtown, the victim of urban renewal, waits to be restored. What is left of the old political landscape vanishes, space by space, but as yet we have no name for the one which is taking form around us.

Roads

I am about to introduce a new and imposing word to the landscape lexicon, and that word is *odology*. It comes from the Greek *hodos*, meaning road or journey. Odology is thus the science or study of roads.

But the question arises: Is *road* the best word we can find? It is very commonplace, and to speak of a science of roads is to imply that the landscape student should be interested in the work of the engineer and matters of construction, alignment, and the efficient movement of goods. Moreover *road* is a relatively new word in English. It became part of the language only in Shakespeare's time, and it first meant nothing more than a journey on horseback. It is still too much of a novelty to have been used in imaginative figures of speech, and no matter how hard we try to give it color, it remains steadfastly prosaic and literal. It would be well if we found a substitute for it. Our way would then be clear to defining *odology* more comprehensively.

And *way* is exactly the word we are seeking! Far older, far more deeply rooted in the language, it has accumulated so many different meanings, is used in so many different metaphors that its original sense of "path" is almost lost. But not entirely. *Way* signifies not only path, but also direction and by extension, intent and manner. We "have our way," we "do things in a way," we follow "a way of life." The phrase "ways and means" suggests that the word can indicate resources at our disposal for attaining an end, and in fact two English words deriving from *hodos* remind us of this: *exodus* means the departure from a place, and *method* (*hodos* is concealed in the second syllable) means a regular or systematic way of accomplishing anything. A way, in short, is a means by which some end, some goal can be reached, and this popular usage undoubtedly accounts for the frequent use of the word for religious beliefs and actions. The Sacred Way (and its innumerable variants) was both a method of spiritual discipline and a road or path leading to a shrine or temple. In the mythical past of Greece the way as symbol and as reality were often indistinguishable. The work of the road builder was seen as dedicated to the gods and was sponsored and directed by priests. According to Greek belief, the gods themselves first traced the alignment of the roads, and Delphi, the center of the cult of Apollo, was never thought of as his home but as the terminus and goal of all the ways he followed. A road which led to a shrine was considered sacred, and no traveler on it was ever molested. Even its margins had a sacred character and were chosen as places of burial. In his account of his travels through Greece in the second century A.D.

Pausanias mentions many times the tombs he saw along the side of the road near cities and country towns.

In those days travelers went more by sea than by land. Greece was a mountainous country with many small ports, and except for a well-made highway between Athens and its port, Piraeus, its roads were often little more than rough trails leading out of the hills to the nearby center, and most of the traffic was on foot. Where there was a shrine or a temple there was almost always a marketplace or agora, usually with a fountain, and so every road or trail ended not only at a sacred place, but in a town where people gathered. The many attributes of Hermes, the god of roads and travelers, tell us something of the several functions of even the smallest of country trails and paths leading to town. As messenger of the gods, Hermes was the witness of treaties and agreements, the guide who conducted the dead to Hades, and the god of the marketplace. His carved image served to indicate boundaries and was frequently seen along country roads, and he was also the protector of doors and entrances. He presided over all gatherings of people, and at the same time he was the god of the pastoral landscape, the protector of flocks and shepherds, and was often depicted as carrying a lamb over his shoulder. By all accounts he was the least warlike of the divinities and was admired less for his strength than for his grace, less for his sense of honor than for his sociable nature. It is not easy to draw any conclusion from this great variety of characteristics, except that it is possible to see Hermes as a link, a mediator between two worlds: the world of the living and that of the dead, the rural world and the urban world, the public space and the secret space of the home. Perhaps we could say that he was the god of *country roads*—roads which shifted location but always eventually led to the temple and the agora; the centripetal roads which farmers and herders use to go to market, where people on foot—pilgrims and merchants and peddlers—travel to their destination. Hermes, the god of mediation, the god of contracts and agreements, seems to symbolize the road as a mean, the way to a chosen end.

When we speculate about the nature of the road in a political landscape we should distinguish between the small, isolated centripetal system, subject to constant change, showing for so little on maps and playing so insignificant a role in the history of material progress, and the impressive, widespread, permanent centrifugal system of highways which we associate with Rome and other empires. Both kinds serve much the same purpose: the strengthening and maintenance of a social order, the tying together at one central place all the spaces which constitute the territory of a community or state, but there are sharp differences between them, not only of scale, but of direction and intent. We have heard so much about the marvels of the Roman system as well as about those of ancient Persia and of the pre-Columbian Incas that it seems scarcely worthwhile discussing them further. Traditional odology, almost exclusively concerned with the technology of roads and their economic function, has taught us to marvel at the thousands of miles of straight, broad, massive construction, the system of rest houses and relay stations, the steady traffic of military formations, officials, messengers going from Rome to distant points in Gaul and Spain and Asia Minor. How often we have been told of the speed of travel over these highways, the splendor of the bridges, and learned of the incredible durability of their paved surfaces—in many places still in use after more than two millennia of service! We have been amazed; but odology properly interpreted implies more than engineering. It implies among other things that there are almost everywhere two parallel systems of roads, one of them local and centripetal, the other regional or national and centrifugal, and we need to recognize the role of both. We need to compare them, particularly when (as in the present case) we are interested in the political complexion of the landscape.

Let me therefore suggest three of the most obvious characteristics of the centrifugal or national highway system, discernable not only in the Roman Empire but in ancient Persia, in the pre-Columbian Inca Empire, even in seventeenth-century France and in contemporary America. Briefly, these are, first, a vastness of scale, second, a disregard of local landscape features, topographical as well as man-made, and last, a persistent emphasis on military and commercial functions. "All roads lead to Rome" is of course a way of saying that Rome is (or was) the supreme destination. But in fact a centrifugal highway system reaching out to control remote areas, important frontier points, as well as fostering commerce with overseas markets always originates in the capital city. In a sense, then, all roads lead *from* Rome, all are built to extend and consolidate the imperial power. The first such highway, the Appian Way, was begun in 312 B.C. as the result of territorial conquest and in order to reach further south. The last highway built by Trajan, four centuries later, was to facilitate the conquest of what is now Rumania.

A golden marker was inserted in the pavement of the Roman Forum to show the spot from which all highways were measured, and handsomely carved milestones gave the name of the highway, the name of the sponsoring authority, and told the distance from that golden marker. In the United States, where we inherited much of the Classical tradition, we too assume that the road or highway—provided it is the creation of the federal government—begins at the center of political power, for there *is* such a marker, though not of gold, on the grounds of the Capitol in Washington, and similar markers are to be found near many state capitols as well.

This exalted origin gives a special quality to the Roman highway, no matter how far it leads into the provinces. It was as if it were superimposed on its rural setting and had no relationship to it. The straightest alignment was the shortest and the one preferred, and so confident were the Roman surveyors and engineers of their ability to overcome almost any topographical obstacle that they laid out their road straight from one point to another, often distant, and thought nothing of crossing marshes by means of solid causeways and slicing through hills. One stretch of a highway in northern Italy went 163 miles with scarcely the slightest deviation. Throughout the whole system there prevailed the same generous dimensions, the same heavy, enduring construction, the same facilities, and the same overwhelming imperial presence, at once reassuring and intimidating.

Consistent with this refusal to compromise with the terrain was the practice of bypassing not only villages but even towns in favor of a more direct route. The royal highway built by the kings of Persia three thousand years ago avoided all provincial centers lest an invading army, using the highway, find stores of arms and supplies, and though in the Roman Empire the highways were available to civilian traffic, local travelers, mostly on foot or horseback, preferred the lateral dirt roads which led to the villages; moreover the system of relay stations and messengers was reserved for government use. The Inca Empire had a remarkably extensive highway system of its own: more than three thousand miles of wonderfully engineered roads and bridges reaching from one end of the territory to the other. But these roads—unpaved because of the total lack of wheeled traffic—were meant for the use of soldiers, officials, and foot messengers, and no one else was allowed to use them.

The notion that certain important highways were meant primarily for the exercise of sovereign authority and to maintain order carried over into America until well into the nineteenth century: soldiers on duty, judges, officials, and clergymen were not obliged to pay toll on the turnpikes, bridges, and ferries.

It seems obvious that when there are restrictions on the use of the centripetal, national highway, or when it is not conveniently located, the rural traveler will devise another way of traveling to the village, and this will consist of paths and trails and primitive roads beaten by local traffic and closely adjusted to the topography and soil, changing when the roads become impassable or according to the season. Thus there evolves what we might call a vernacular road system: flexible, without overall plan, but definitely centripetal; a system which is isolated, usually without maintenance, and the bane of long-range travelers and of a government wanting to expedite military or commercial traffic. So it is only a matter of time before the local system is taken in hand and coordinated with the national network—usually much to the distress of the small community involved.

Rome was probably the first state to plan new rural road systems, and the outcome was an extensive artificial political landscape which has served as a model for many modern plans. As the Republic and later the Empire expanded, it found itself engaged in the settling of new or vacated territories

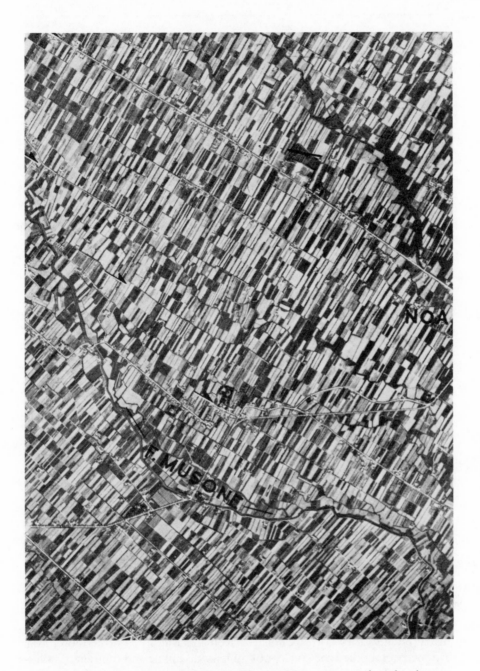

Northern Italy, between Padua and Treviso. The river Musone acts as a boundary between the centuriated territoria of two Roman towns, with their road-grids oriented differently. The modern roads are south of the Musone. (British Crown Copyright Reserved)

and in the establishing of communities of small farmers. The usual procedure was to divide the publicly owned lands into large squares of about 120 acres, called *centuriae*, of a little less than a half mile to the side. Some of these resettlement or settlement projects were small, but as John Bradford writes in his book on aerial archeology, "the first and fundamental impression that we receive from the system spread across North Italy is the magnitude of the conception that inspired their construction, and the blend of ambition and stubborn capability in matters of detail that could give effect to it. Virtually it would have been possible to ride from Turin to Trieste—a distance of 300 miles from west to east—within centuriated systems all the way."[9]

What concerns us in the system is the function of the road. Each of these *centuriae*, or rectangles, was divided into farms varying in size between 25 and 100 acres, depending on soil, topography, and the legislation creating the project. The *centuriae* were bounded by roads, and the whole landscape was a grid system of straight roads, usually bordered by irrigation ditches, hedges, and trees, and crossing at right angles.

Most of these farms raised wheat, grapes, and assorted fruits and vegetables, all of which they sold in the nearest *colonia*, or planned town; and farms of this sort needed a road system not only to reach their fields and orchards and transport the produce to market, but as a sort of permanent, large-scale framework for the irrigation ditches. The roads appear to have been well constructed and carefully classified as to width and type of use: the *iter*, or footpath, 2 feet wide, the *actus*, or cattle drive, 4 feet wide, and the *via*, or vehicular road, 8 feet wide. The nucleus of the landscape was the point of intersection of two highways, the *decumanus maximus* (east–west) and the *cardo maximus* (north–south), and it was here that a town was usually built.

The choosing of this spot had in the remote past been a solemn ceremony. "For the Etruscans [the axial system] incorporated the relation between terrestrial delimitation and the celestial *templum*. The heavens were like a circle divided in four parts by two axes. The *cardine* and *decumanus* as employed in city planning were an earthly representation of the heavenly pattern."[10] Germanic folklore likewise attached great religious importance to the crossroads as a place of justice or retribution. But by the time the Romans were laying out the centuriated landscape the symbolic meaning of the intersection of those two highways was pretty well forgotten, and in fact it was the military encampment rather than the image of a celestial temple that served as a model for the new towns. "The Roman urban planner," Castagnoli remarks, "was little moved by celestial speculation and adopted the principles of axial symmetry because they corresponded to Roman taste. . . . Furthermore, axial symmetry embodied the concept of military discipline and centralized political power, focusing the city upon a single point, where the magistrate exercised his authority."[11]

So the *colonia*, the chief town in each of these artificial landscapes, played a

prosaic role: it was the place of the market, the place of government administration, the place of justice—all of them centered around that important
intersection in a rectangular forum. The whole system of land distribution
had two characteristics worth bearing in mind, for they distinguish the Roman grid landscape from our own, despite the obvious similarities between
the two: the Roman landscape was focused on a centrally located town,
whereas our grid system never included any provision for urban settlements.
Second, the Roman land holdings were based on a traditional stabilized type
of farming (or gardening) and a traditional size, appropriate to family exploitation and the use of a yoke of oxen. The American system on the contrary
stipulated only a *minimum* size for the individual holding and implied no
particular kind of agriculture. Thus the Roman landscape was intended for a
special kind of citizen: the citizen as small landholder, farmer, soldier (or
veteran), taxpayer, attached to his piece of land and dependent on the urban
center. The road system helped maintain that identity. Unlike the roads in
nucleated or clustered farm villages that lead out to the pastures and fields
and other places of more or less solitary, routine work, the roads in the
centuriated landscape lead from the independent homestead to the town with
its market, its forum, its religious ceremonies and monuments, its political
life. And the road itself was often a place of social behavior; most travel was
on foot; the roadside shrines and monuments, the frequent intersections, the
houses flanking it, the shade of the trees, and the flowing irrigation ditches—
all gave it animation.

But the importance of the road in the political landscape reminds us of
something we are not always willing to accept: man as a political animal is
always inclined to be footloose, inclined to leave family and home for a more
stimulating place. As inhabitants of the earth we like to put our roots down
and to *belong* to a certain spot, never to move again; the road or highway is a
menace. Yet that other, political identity urges us to leave and to seek out the
locus of action and discourse. Town, where we become citizens and can be
seen, begins directly outside our door, where the road stands for public life.
If, as the Greeks believed, the gods in their wandering made the first roads,
then I daresay it is an act of piety to follow in their footsteps, and politically
speaking, the best of all landscapes, the best of all roads, are those which
foster movement toward a desirable social goal. But that is something for the
odologist to decide.

Spaces, Sacred and Profane

Wherever we go in the contemporary landscape we run across these signs:
boundaries, roads, and places of assembly. We read them at once, and we not
only read them, we create them ourselves, almost without realizing that
without them we could not function as members of society. To me this

universal need—and universal ability—to organize space, to divide it into microspaces, assemble them into macrospaces, is impressive evidence that there is a common, unchanging human nature. But each age, each society develops its own unique kind of spatial organization. There are societies which cannot rest until they have defined every space, natural or man-made, in conveniently human or political categories. If, for instance, there is a river, it is immediately thought of in terms of navigation or water power. If there are mountains they are to be used for defense or grazing or the providing of wood, and if there is open country, it is to be divided up into farms and home lots and given a system of roads.

The message here is that in the political landscape the natural environment has no inherent identity of its own; it is simply a means to an end, a human end, and space is consequently organized so that every group, every activity has its own well-defined space. Aristotle said that in the Agora the older people and the younger people were to have their own separate places for exercising: not because there was danger of friction between the generations; on the contrary, if they shared a space they might merge and become indistinguishable.

Differences in spatial organization are largely a matter of how we happen to classify things and occupations and people, and separate them. There are societies where all garden plants are grown together though great distinctions will be made as to who eats what. There are societies where the house is simply one large room. And, in fact, we notice that we ourselves are beginning to ignore some traditional divisions. There was a time, about a century ago, when the introduction of a separate room for eating, a dining room, was considered a triumph of civilization. But now we usually eat and cook and watch television in the same place. We are trying to eliminate racial and class divisions in our cities, and we talk about a national forest as "a land of many uses," meaning that it can be used for recreation and lumbering and grazing and wildlife preservation. More and more we are turning away from the old concepts and trying to discover a harmonious relationship with *natural* spaces, spaces defined by climate or topography. Yet we can never entirely do without the human basis of spatial organization, for there will be times and places where the space itself is less important than the content, where space simply plays the role of background.

In that pattern of spaces we call a landscape, particularly a rural landscape, the most common, the most elementary space is that small piece of land where a family lives and works. Every other space is a modification or an extension of it. In the political landscape we learn to perceive it as the prototypal minispace. For the assumption (based less on history than on theory) is that in the beginning each family received a piece of land large enough to provide it with a living and roughly equal in value to every other piece. This piece of land we even today call "a lot," a usage harking back to an age when the distribution was made by the drawing of lots. But whereas to us distribution of that kind seems governed entirely by chance, there was a time when it seemed a divine dispensation, the decision of some god. "The lot by which [the holdings] were distributed," Plato tells us, "is a god. . . . You may choose or decline to take part in the distribution, but if you do take part you . . . must acknowledge that the land is sacred to all the gods . . . and anyone buying and selling his allotted land or house must suffer the penalty appropriate to the crime."[12]

The once prevalent notion that land was never to be alienated but was to remain in possession of the family forever is a reminder that there is (or was) a religious landscape or at least a religious interpretation of landscape formation. In *The Ancient City* Fustel de Coulanges ascribes the existence and importance of landed private property to the old practice of burying the family dead in the fields of the farm, making them in effect sacred spaces. But in the strictly theoretical landscape of antiquity this explanation was discounted, and other more secular justifications for the persistence of the family-sized farm were found. The farm was essential (many believed) simply because it produced food and enabled the family to survive. It was desirable chiefly from the economic point of view. A more thoughtful explanation was that the farmer, because of his work outdoors, was likely to be a good soldier, strong and inured to hardship. A third point of view, popular among statesmen and philosophers, and probably based on observation, was that the family-sized farm produced men who were not only physically but also mentally qualified to serve as soldiers, for they were usually steady, methodical, and little given to political agitation—not rebelling as long as their existence was bearable.

It is from Aristotle that we derive our idealized version of the small landowner as a model of civic virtue. "When the farming element, being in possession of a moderate amount of property, is the predominant section, the work of the constitution goes on in accordance with the laws; because so long as they work they have enough to live on, but they cannot take time off in order to hold office, so they install the law as a guiding principle and themselves only attend the necessary meetings of the Assembly of the people";[13] and again: "An agricultural population makes the best demos. . . . For having no great abundance of wealth they are kept busy and rarely attend the Assembly; on the other hand being constantly at work in the fields they do not lack the necessities. So they do not covet other's possessions . . . . Moreover to have the power to vote at elections makes up any deficiency which those who have political ambitions may feel."[14]

The virtues identified with this middling way of life, halfway between the aristocratic and the rootless existences of the urban proletariat, are essentially domestic: the ability to manage the household, to give orders to the slaves or laborers; self-reliance, respect for tradition, respect for the rights of neighbors. The civic role of the small independent farmer is limited to his wise and moderate involvement in village affairs; the urban assembly is not his realm. If he is called upon to serve as a soldier it is because as a free man and citizen he is entitled to possess arms and has a vested interest in the defense of the state; physical prowess has little to do with his qualifications. Thus the earlier idea that the farmer was a good soldier because he was a hard worker is modified; he is now valued for his moral qualities, and indeed he is all the better suited for public affairs for leaving the heavy work to slaves and spending his leisure in self-improvement.

The family holding is thus a miniature state, neither too large nor too small for its purpose. It is surrounded by a very visible wall or by rows of trees, it is near enough the road to be in touch with the community, and yet it is distinctly and forever separate. It is a territory with its own domestic hier-archy, its own ancestors, its own divinities to be venerated on special days and in special places. It enforces its own code of conduct, its own traditional relationships, generation after generation, but at the same time is much concerned with keeping its image honored and respected by the outside world. This unit is, in theory at least, only large enough to occupy two able-bodied men, father and son, and only one yoke of oxen; though in fact many such family units were far larger and more luxurious, and the owners in consequence more powerful political figures. Ruskin paints an attractive pic-ture of what he supposes that Classical landscape to have been. After men-tioning how Classical descriptions of landscape reveal its "subservience to human comfort, to the foot, the taste, the smell," and their "excessive sim-ilarity" he concludes that the most perfect spot would be a garden

> where the principal ideas are . . . order, symmetry, and fruitfulness; the beds being duly ranged between rows of vines, which, as well as the pear, apple, and fig trees, bear fruit continually, some grapes being yet sour, while others are getting black; there are plenty of "*orderly* square beds of herbs," chiefly leeks, and two fountains, one running through the garden, and one under the pavement of the palace to a reservoir for the citizens. . . . In all this I cannot too strongly mark the utter absence of any trace of the feeling for what we call the picturesque, and the constant dwelling . . . on what was available, pleasant, or useful.

Ruskin then adds a scornful comment on the "blundering, pseudo-pictur-esque, pseudo-classical minds of Claude and the Renaissance landscape painters."[15]

He is in one respect quite right, for Renaissance landscape paintings ignore the small farm almost completely. Yet every society which organizes space in political terms tries, with varying success, to create and preserve those small, not very productive pieces of private property. If (as eventually happens) they are devoured by speculators and large landowners, or if they are abandoned by their families in favor of the city, their image is kept alive in literature. Virgil wrote beautifully of life on the hereditary farm, and so did Horace.

Cicero spoke in defense of the few remaining Sicilian farmers—"Those whose means of tillage consist of one yoke of oxen, who labor on their farms with their own hands"—and Cincinnatus, who reluctantly left his small farm and a frugal existence to become dictator, was of course not only a Roman hero but the archetypal farmer-as-citizen. Even Vitruvius, writing at a time when large estates were replacing the small farms, pays lip service to the tradition of rustic simplicity and independence.

Here is John Adams repeating Classical saws: "The only possible way then of preserving public virtue is to make the acquisition of land easy to every member of society: to make the division of land into small quantities, so that the multitudes may be possessed of landed estates."

And Jefferson with his colleagues then produced a political landscape faithful to Classical theory: a vast grid system, a nationwide (or almost nationwide) composition of squares. Though not specifically designed to be divided into small holdings for those whom Jefferson described as God's "peculiar deposit for substantial and genuine virtues"—farmers, that is to say—it encourages their formation, and as the Midwest becomes populated and flourishes as an agricultural countryside, America is pleased to see the unfolding of a landscape dedicated to civic virtue. "The farmer is the most noble and independent man in society," an agricultural editor declared in 1841. "He has ever been honored and respected from the days of Cincinnatus, the Roman farmer."

But as is often the case, literature and political oratory were behind the times, eulogizing a landscape feature which was already on its way out. Public opinion was beginning to soft-pedal the importance of virtue on the family farm and indeed to depoliticize the whole new landscape. The small, independent farmstead was instead seen as a bulwark against the expansion of slavery or as an outlet for the urban poor or as providing the western railroad lines with customers and traffic, and today those who promote it do so because (we are told) it is healthy and inexpensive or because it can produce certain labor intensive goods which the large commercial farmers cannot cultivate with profit or because a landscape of small farms, each with a tree-embowered homestead, is a valuable amenity. Social or economic or ecological arguments, not political arguments, are thus the ones we use in discussing the family farm. Those who criticize it, engineers and agronomists, say that it is too small to be efficient in this day of expensive farm equipment: radical political theory condemns it as a reactionary stronghold of bourgeois individualism, sociologists point to the poverty and hopelessness of the average small farm, particularly in the South. There are even environmentalists who warn us that we can no longer leave the management of our countryside to small farmers, desperately producing larger and larger crops regardless of the long-range ecological costs.

Perhaps our dilemma comes in part from the fact that we still think of the family farm in terms of traditional visibility and permanence: a farm of permanent size with a permanent homestead and a permanent type of agriculture: a reassuringly stable element in the landscape, always easy to identify. But is there no other way of envisaging it? Fraser Hart suggests that we abandon the idea that the family farm is always owned by the farmer, that it is always a homogeneous unit, that it always produces the same crops: those were Classical criteria, no longer applicable.

> A family farm is simply an operating unit which provides an adequate level of living for the labor of a father and son, with a hired hand at certain stages of the demographic cycle. . . . Neither size nor ownership are stipulated in this system. . . . No matter what the farming system, the amount of land which was large enough for a family farm a generation ago has become, or is becoming, too small, and the size of the operating unit must be enlarged. . . . The farmer who rents the land he needs to expand his operation, in order to keep his family farm from degenerating into an undersized unit, often discovers that tenancy is not so bad after all.[16]

But Plato would not have approved.

Visibility

Several times in discussing the political landscape I have mentioned the importance of visibility. In our context, the word means of course something more than that an object can be seen. It means that it is conspicuous, that it is distinct from its surroundings, and that as a form it can be understood at a glance; and in this sense it is obvious that not all objects in the landscape are really visible. To the environmentalist the topography and vegetation have visibility; to the student of architecture it will be the buildings; all the rest is merely background, and all objects in that background seem to merge into a kind of invisibility.

The student of the political landscape will look for a special kind of visibility, and what that is likely to be we learn from the writings of Pausanias, whom I have mentioned once before. He indicates very clearly what the political—or Classical—observer perceives as visible and what can be ignored. As he traveled through second-century Greece, conscientiously going from town to town to learn what he could about each of them, the things that caught his eye were almost exclusively man-made. He described the roadside monuments and tombs, the walls built around cities, the processional streets leading to the agora or acropolis. He examined every shrine, statue, temple, public building, visited every acropolis where monuments were to be found. He visited the theater and the stadium and the agora itself.

He did this not as amateur of art or even as an antiquarian; he did it because these were the only objects with what to him was visibility. The impression of the ancient Greek landscape that we get from Pausanias is fragmentary and from our point of view hopelessly incomplete. What does he have to say about the layout of the city, about the places where people live and work and play, about everyday existence? What does he tell us about the natural landscape of mountains and seacoast he spent so much time traveling through, or about the well-populated rural countryside? The visibility we look for in vain in Classical accounts is given us in a succinct and vivid form in the words of a modern historical geographer.

> In the fifth century the typical [Greek] city was still but a jumble of narrow winding streets and one-storeyed houses amid which lay somewhat incongruously the agora, or market place, and the public buildings upon which it had perhaps lavished a large amount of its income. It was, in fact, little more than an overgrown village. Even Athens had its slums. "The city itself," wrote the Pseudo-Dicaearchus, "is dry and ill-supplied with water. The streets are nothing but miserable old lanes, the houses mean, with a few better ones among them." The majority of the houses consisted of a single room, with floor of beaten clay and walls of sun-dried bricks. In the case of Athens the oldest and poorest housing lay nearest to the Acropolis.[17]

What *we* find important in the city is the social or sociological. We have become almost blind to the political: to those spaces and structures which Pausanias identified with the permanent and public aspects of the community, its political symbols. He gives us a landscape punctuated, as it were, by a number of separate, more or less isolated "timeless" forms and spaces—forms and spaces, moreover, that reinforce status rather than serve a function.

In his discussion of Classical (or political) space Spengler remarks that

> the Classical statue in its splendid bodiliness—all structure and expressive surfaces and no incorporeal *arrière pensée* whatsoever—contains without remainder all that Actuality is for the Classical eye. The Classical universe, the *Cosmos* or well-ordered aggregate of all near and completely viewable things, is concluded by the corporeal vault of heaven. . . . The State is a body which is made up of all the bodies of its citizens, the law knows only corporeal persons and material things. And the feeling finds its last and noblest expression in the stone body of the Classical Temple.[18]

We could scarcely accuse the political landscape of the early United States or even that of seventeenth-century France of making a cult of the body. But the isolated, domineering public building or monument certainly found favor in both countries, and both resembled the Classical prototype in their design and use of space to indicate status: what better expression of an egalitarian political ideal than the uniform squares of our grid landscape and our grid cities? It is in this kind of political spatial organization that the boundary plays so significant a role. As I have suggested, the political function of the boundary is not to define a homogeneous area but to protect the object which it surrounds. To repeat, the political (as distinguished from the social or topographical) boundary is *not* a tight-fitting epidermis, it is a loose-fitting envelope, a way of giving a visible, corporeal identity to a temple, a city, a state. Wycherley speaks of the walls surrounding Greek communities as being "loosely flung around a city; it was not the frame into which the rest was fitted, and it was not normally a dominant factor in the plan."[19] And in fact these walls were sometimes so extensive that they could not be adequately manned by the population. They were, in short, visible confirmation of the permanence and sanctity of the city, so much so that Plato in *The Laws* proposed that all the dwellings in his Utopian city should be part of the city wall. "If men are to have a city wall at all, the private houses should be constructed right from the foundations so that the whole city forms in effect a single wall. . . . A whole city looking like a single wall will be quite a pretty sight."[20]

No doubt; instead of being a haphazard collection of private, temporary, changeable dwellings it would be a permanent and visible element in the political landscape.

One last word on the ancient significance of boundaries. In the "regions" of Rome, the ancient administrative subdivisions of the city, "the areas were not defined in terms of dimensions, now the practice though never customary in Antiquity or in the Middle Ages, but in terms of their perimeters"[21]— in other words in terms of their boundaries, their visible features.

Do we need to be reminded of how over the last hundred years the American landscape has destroyed the political organization of space in favor of an economic or ecological organization? Of how we have managed to desanctify and destabilize space and liberate it from its two-dimensional constraints? We have only to look around us to see what has happened. I am thinking in particular of the current generation of environmental designers, who are very much aware of the spatial revolution, inspired by it, and yet uncertain of how to express it. To many of them (judging more from what they say and write than from what they actually do) it is much as if traditional visible spaces were being swallowed up by an endless, timeless invisible Superspace, so that all they can think about is not space itself but how we react to it: how we perceive it, how we behave in it, how ideas are diffused in it; spatial simulation models, the semiotics of space, space and phenomenology. In time these speculations will bear fruit. But they are not yet helpful to the layman, who still hankers after visible evidence of the changes in store for us all. That is why it is useful to study spatial organizations in other societies and at other times: not to imitate them but to learn that in the field of landscapes, what we see, what we have understood, what we enjoy all count for a great deal in how we organize space ourselves.

From that point of view the political landscape, even though obsolete, has several things in its favor. When, for instance, spaces—whether public or private—are meant to last and to be looked at they are likely to be given an agreeable, easily apprehended shape: preferably square, if not, rectangular; and when that is not possible, then at least chunky; thickset and clear as to form and always well defined. Perhaps that is one reason for the Greeks preferring—at least after the fifth century—the grid plan city; the neat array of uniform, rectangular blocks made the composition easy to interpet as a visible unit. We might recall that our own Continental Congress stipulated in 1780—well before the creation of the national grid system of square town-ships—that all new states were to measure "not less than one hundred and fifty miles square, or as near thereto as circumstances permit." Even now, when boundaries have no great symbolic value, Frenchmen derive satisfac-tion from the beautifully hexagonal shape of their country.

Still, there are other than esthetic grounds for cherishing the visibility of a space. Spaces have a way of underscoring or calling attention to their con-tent. "Property makes the man visible and accessible. I cannot see a man's mind or his character. But when I see what he has chosen and what he does with it, I know what he likes, and quite a good deal about his principles."[22]

This sounds a little like nineteenth-century Illinois: Farmer Thrifty stand-ing proudly in front of his big red barn. But it probably had its equivalent in Attica and Republican Rome and perhaps in ancient China too. In those vanished landscapes there must have been the same well-kept farms, neither too large nor too small, the same tight-knit, hardworking families, the same countryside of square fields; everything square in all senses of the word, with every good quality and every limitation associated with squareness.

We are well aware that this landscape has all but seen its day, and not a few are glad to see the last of it; we find it too commonplace for greatness. Perhaps; but whatever the shapes and spaces and patterns predominating in the American landscape of the future there will surely come a time when we will learn to perceive those spaces as symbols of continuity and order, and when our eye suddenly rediscovers in them landscape beauty of the elemental kind that transcends history.

On the Road

The best known of highway systems is the one which evolved in France in the seventeenth and eighteenth centuries. Here, for the first time, we meet with a well-defined program of road building to serve both the political and eco-nomic interests of a nation. The vast and impressive system of highways, most of them centered on Paris, linked important agricultural regions with ports and the centers of distribution, and at the same time established the authority of the king and his army in remote and sometimes rebellious regions.

The physical features of the French highway system are worth noting, for they not only resemble in many respects those of the Roman and Persian and Inca systems, but suggest how we might possibly classify roads in terms of their impact on the social order. The first step in the planning of the pre-revolutionary network was to define the right of way: to lay out broad, straight roads with wide, open margins; and whereas most local travel was confined to the rivers and valleys where the villages were located, the new highways deliberately followed the crests of hills and the higher elevations. This for three reasons: the soil here was firmer and less disturbed by floods and marshes, highways located on the heights were less likely to become involved in local traffic and problems of expropriation of farmland; and finally, they were more visible. The parallel rows of poplars which the authorities planted became conspicuous elements in the landscape and reminded everyone of the power of the crown. Only within the last generation have we come to recognize the beauty of these broad, straight highways, undulating over the hills and open country, with their perspective of trees; and though the romantic nineteenth century found them monotonous and artificial and empty of life, the French government has recently declared some of these highways national monuments.

Since it was not the intention of these royal roads to serve the small communities in the valleys, they had little or no connection with the surrounding rural landscape. The sparse traffic on the highways was composed of coaches, caravans of wholesale merchants, military and official travelers, whereas in the nearby countryside, a totally different kind of activity prevailed. A French geographer describes the situation in the eighteenth century:

> The villages are isolated, the roads in a bad state, poorly laid out or even entirely lacking. The bridges are in ruins, the farm produce cannot be moved, whereas elsewhere there is a lack of food. . . . The local road system, the instinctive and anonymous work of generations . . . covers the countryside with a maze of innumerable roads, paths, and trails. The royal highways pass through, sometimes destroying the network, sometimes using it, at times avoiding it and crossing deserted moors or forests empty of inhabitants, at others bypassing populated regions, villages, even large towns and small cities which are obliged to link up to the royal highways by means of makeshift roads.[23]

These royal highways—Roman, Persian, Inca, French—have in common a preference for the straight perspective, disregarding topography for greater visibility and a shorter alignment. They bypass or avoid the local landscapes and their communities and head straight for the political or commercial or military destination. All of them, in one manner or another, restrict their traffic to a small and powerful group of users—either by edict, by accessibility, or by their destination. We are likely to compare our own interstate system to the system of royal highways, and there are obvious similarities. But I suspect that an odologist would put the interstate in a very different category and point out that it was never intended as a political device to reinforce or change the social order.

How does a highway system accomplish these objectives? It can bring people together and create something like a public place for face-to-face interaction and discussion. Those royal highways made it easy only for a certain class in society to come together: officials and political, religious, and military leaders: they could meet and transact public business at selected centers; mobility thus fostered the growth of an effective and powerful ruling group. But the rank and file, particularly those in the countryside, were doomed to immobility and to political inaction.

So an essential element in any healthy political landscape is the network of neighborhood or rural roads. This truth is strangely ignored by scholars. In a typical regional geography you will rarely run across any lengthy discussion of the local road system. Bad roads, we are constantly (and rightly) informed, handicap the economy; but we could also define a bad road as one which leads only to the place of work or one which makes sociability difficult or unrewarding; a bad road, speaking in odological terms, is one which provides us with no sense of rewarding destination.

The United States offers one of the largest and most ambitious examples of a nation once so politically minded that it was determined that every citizen, every landowner should have easy access to a road leading to the political center. We can still see the results of that policy, now unfortunately neglected, in the grid system.

Altogether the grid system covers two-thirds of the United States; all except the thirteen original states, Kentucky, and parts of Ohio and Georgia. It divides the country into square miles, or sections, and these are in turn combined into townships of thirty-six sections. One of the distinctive features of the system is that every section, every square mile, is in theory bordered on all four sides by public roads. In practice there are vast areas in the West where no such roads exist; but there is legal provision for creating them if and when that becomes necessary.

The purpose of these roads—which in the beginning were totally unimproved and almost nonexistent—was to provide every landowner with a means to get to the nearest town in order to vote, pay taxes, go to church, go to court, attend lectures—most of these being political errands. Eventually these roads were reinterpreted in economic terms: as leading to market or to a shipping point, and that is the way we still think of them. A farm to market road is an extremely useful thing, but it is not the same as a farm to country courthouse road.

We know that parts of the back country of the United States are not very lively. Many houses have been abandoned or are being used as barns for baled alfalfa; farms have been consolidated. The back roads, heirs of the grid system of almost two hundred years ago, are usually unpaved. They stretch straight ahead, up and down hill, mile after mile; dusty, unbeautiful, punctuated by tipsy mailboxes and sagging telephone lines; but not quite lifeless, because

Dirt road near Paoli, Pennsylvania. (Photo: Gordon Parks)

every county commissioner, every selectman knows that the roads in his territory have to be graded—especially near election time—have to have the borrow pits cleaned, have to be passable for the mail carrier and the school bus. The heaps of tumbleweed are bulldozed aside; the snow is pushed into the margins, and the mail carrier in his four-wheel drive goes through in order to thrust into the rare mailboxes an ad for a tire sale at Firestone, a mail-order catalog, and a tax bill.

Maintaining these back roads is expensive and never-ending, and local authorities would like nothing better than to have most of them discontinued. In time the last stubborn farm couple, the last family of transient farm workers will move out. But until that happens the roads will persist, and as an admirer of the political features of the American landscape, I rejoice in their survival. The sight of a yellow road grader blundering down a country road signifies that no matter how far we may live from town and a paved highway, no matter how poor and insignificant, we are still bona fide members of society, political animals for all our loneliness. Let the county spend good money operating the grader up to my mailbox! That is what our taxes are for!

The Other Landscape

Before we take leave of the political landscape, the landscape designed to produce law-abiding citizens, honest officials, eloquent orators, and patriotic soldiers, let us have a final glimpse of it. Here is a description or survey of Italy in the last years of the Roman Empire, written in the third century A.D. by Tertullian, one of the greatest of early Christian writers. The irony of the passage is that while it seems to assume that the civilized world will endure forever, it was actually composed about a century before the barbarians invaded the Empire and destroyed that particular landscape and substituted another, quite different one.

> All places are now accessible, all are well known, all open to commerce; most pleasant farms have obliterated all traces of what were once dreary and dangerous wastes; cultivated fields have subdued forests; flocks and herds have expelled wild beasts; sandy deserts are sown; rocks are planted; marshes are drained; and where once were hardly solitary cottages, there are now large cities. No longer are [savage] islands dreaded, nor their rocky shores feared; everywhere are houses, and inhabitants, and settled government, and civilized life.

Some of the features which Tertullian thinks well of are precisely those which environmentalists condemn: forests replaced by plowed fields, wildlife destroyed, marshes drained, cities taking the place of wilderness, and all parts of the countryside accessible to commerce. It is certainly not an exciting landscape; it may even have been monotonous. Yet it must have been impressive; for it made visible two qualities very uncommon in those remote times and by no means universal even now: order and prosperity. It was a *livable* landscape, it was an achievement, socially speaking; and what I am here concerned with is not the landscape which the artist or geographer or archeologist finds unique, but the landscape which shows us how people try to strike a balance between their need to get along with one another and their need to adjust to the environment, and survive. We never completely succeed and often overdo the human aspect of the problem. But we cannot overlook the fact that almost every utopian version of a more perfect world starts out by proposing a political infrastructure—the equitable division of land, the town as center of government, the defensible boundary. All social philosophers from Plato to Thomas More to Lewis Mumford have stipulated those landscape features. I am no admirer of utopian writing, yet insofar as each of us is, to a greater or lesser degree, a political animal, we respond to utopian ideals: the family farm, the dignified place of public assembly and interaction; and we like to think of boundaries and divisions protecting small communities and insuring justice.

Only when we think about the private, the more emotional side of existence do we find something missing in the political landscape. It is time therefore to explore that alternative landscape, the one in which we feel at home as inhabitants of the earth. The contrast between the two is clear: man, the political animal, thinks of the landscape as his own creation, as belonging to him; thinks of it as a well-defined territory or domain which confers on him a status totally distinct from that of all other creatures; whereas man the inhabitant sees the landscape as a habitat which was there long before he appeared. He sees himself as belonging to the landscape in the sense that he is its product. Yet the two points of view have this in common: they see the landscape as something shared; they assume that human beings cannot survive and fulfill themselves unless there is a landscape to hold them together in a group.

If we were to ask ourselves why we believed that we were inhabitants of the earth we would have little trouble finding an answer: we belong here because human beings are part of the natural order, related to all other forms of life, responding to much the same laws, and no less dependent on a healthy and diverse environment. This condition of being part of nature brings with it certain responsibilities and restraints. To damage a system which allows an infinite number of life forms to coexist, to destroy what we cannot possibly replace, would not only be irresponsible, it would threaten our own survival. Therefore, the first of our obligations is to discover the laws of nature and follow them; we can then lead secure and creative lives and contribute to the well-being of the earth and its inhabitants. Then to show our dedication we would tell what we had been doing to save energy, protect wildlife, raise organic vegetables, and how we had been practicing handicrafts and following certain spiritual disciplines.

This would be an honest answer, but not in itself much of a philosophical statement. It merely implies that if we want to survive (never mind what for) we had better obey the rules of the game. But as we know, there are other, more earnest ways of justifying our close relationship with and dependence on the natural environment. It is typical of our times that we turn for an answer to the psychologist, the ecologist, not the theologian. It is also typical that we are more concerned with establishing a harmonious and fruitful relation with nature in its broadest sense than with the landscape, which in the not so distant past was the site of lifelong daily contact with the natural world. We use the somewhat shopworn phrase *child of nature* to indicate the desired status and way of life. But long before there was such a concept as *nature* (which in the current sense of country as opposed to the town dates from the late eighteenth century) the phrase most used was *child of the earth*.

We are most of us familiar with the myth identifying the earth as the mother of all forms of life. This is no mere figure of speech as when we refer to our country as the motherland or to our college as alma mater. On the contrary, the myth makes it plain that the first human beings came out of the womb of the Earth Mother. Among the Pueblo Indians of the Southwest there are several versions of this Emergence Myth: they all tell of two sisters who dwelt in a dark water cave until a godlike emissary—sometimes the Spider Woman, the link between worlds—showed them how to emerge from their cave into the world of trees and grass and wait for the sun to come up. In the Pueblo of Acoma the account reads, "[T]hey came out of the earth, from Iyatiku, the mother. They came out through a hole in the north called Shipap. They crawled out like grasshoppers; their bodies were naked and soft. It was all dark; the sun had not yet risen."[24] "That human beings are the offspring of the earth is a world-wide article of faith," Mircea Eliade writes.

> In many languages man is called "born of the earth." Let us choose a few random examples. The Armenians call the Earth "the maternal womb, from which issued men." In numerous languages man is called "born of the earth." . . . Among the Peruvians the earth is called Earth Mother. It is believed that children come "from the depths of the Earth," from caves, grottos, crevices, but also from marshes and springs and streams. Every region of Europe, almost every town or village knows of a rock or spring which brings children.

He adds:

> We must be on our guard not to think of these superstitions or metaphors as meant only for children. Reality is more complex. Until recently there persisted among Europeans the obscure awareness of a mystic solidarity with the land of one's birth. It was not a commonplace love of country or province; it was not admiration of a familiar landscape or veneration of ancestors buried, generation after generation, around the village church. It was something entirely different: the mystic experience of autochthony, of being indigenous, the profound sense of having emerged from the local ground, the sense that the earth had given birth to us, much as it had given birth, in its inexhaustible fertility, to rocks and streams and flowers. . . . The obscure memory of a pre-existence in the womb of the earth has had significant consequences. It has produced among men and women a feeling of cosmic relatedness to the environment; one could even say that at one period men were less aware of belonging to the human species than of a kind of cosmic-biologic participation in the life of their landscape. . . . This sort of experience produced a mystic link with *place,* whose intensity is still echoed in folklore and popular tradition. But this mystic solidarity was not without consequences. It prevented among men the feeling of being *creators.* In legitimizing his children who "arrived" from some part of the Cosmos, the father did not have children of his own, properly speaking, only new members of the family, new implements for work.[25]

Two items in these remarks of Eliade's are worth pondering when we speculate about the kind of landscape created by man the inhabitant: the first is the assumption, persuasive but of course impossible to verify, that early men adopted an essentially passive attitude toward all aspects of creation and saw themselves simply as recipients of Mother Earth's bounty. The second, much more significant, is this: that our fundamental relationship with the natural environment was strictly confined to *one* place, *one* familiar ancestral landscape and in no way included the whole earth or even the neighboring landscape. Our own landscape was unique in its sacred origin, and we in consequence among all peoples were unique.

Natural Spaces

These two landscapes—the political and the one which for brevity's sake I call the inhabited landscape—in real life are always found together. As a usual thing the political landscape is on a larger, more impressive scale, more permanent and easier to spot, whereas the inhabited landscape is likely to be poor and small and hard to find. But both of them, in one degree or another, are always there, and it is only when we discuss them in the abstract that we are able to separate them.

Yet they *do* differ, and not only in appearance or what for the lack of a better term I refer to as spatial organization, but in their underlying purpose, and I would tentatively say that while the political landscape is deliberately *created* in order to make it possible for men to live in a just society, the inhabited landscape merely *evolves* in the course of our trying to live on harmonious terms with the natural world surrounding us. I would add that this second kind of landscape is much the older and still the most common; indeed I believe it is once again coming into fashion as more and more of us feel a new attachment to the natural order. The attitude of the Navaho is that "on the road of life to his final destiny, which will make man one with the universe, he is concerned with maintaining harmony with all things, with subsistence and the orderly replenishment of his own kind."[26] This philosophy, expressed in scientific terms, is far from alien to that of many contemporary environmentalists. It is when we try translating the point of view into a landscape that difficulties arise. For there are many different kinds of inhabited landscapes, different ways of adjusting to the natural order, just as there are many different kinds of political landscapes. The one which concerns us here is totally unlike the landscape of the nomadic Navahos, for it is the product of untold generations of farmers equipped with axes and plows and their own notions of how to adapt to the natural environment. In his analysis of what he calls the Gemeinschaft (or the traditional pretechnological community) the German sociologist Tönnies provides us with a glimpse of the traditional inhabited landscape of Europe of say four centuries ago.

> The people see themselves surrounded by the inhabited earth. It seems as if, in the beginning of time, the earth itself had brought forth from its womb the human beings who look upon her as their mother. The land supports their tents and houses, and the more durable the houses become, the more men become attached to their own ground, however limited. The relationship grows stronger and deeper when the land is cultivated. With the plow furrowing the soil, nature is tamed just as the animals of the woods are domesticated. But this is only the result of the ever-renewed efforts of countless generations where every step in progress is handed

down from father to son. The area settled and occupied is therefore a common heritage, the land of the ancestors toward which all feel and act as descendants and blood brothers. In this sense, it can be regarded as a living substance which, with its spiritual or psychological values, persists in the everlasting flux of its elements, viz., the human beings. . . . Habit, next to the ties of blood, forms the strongest bond among contemporaries, and likewise, memory links the living to the dead. The homeland, as the embodiment of dear memories, holds the heart of man, who parts from it with sorrow and looks back to it with homesickness and longing from abroad. . . . Even in times of nomadic wandering, family and home are the source of such sentiment. . . . The metaphysical character of the clan, the tribe, the village and town community is, so to speak, wedded to the land in a lasting union.[27]

For most of us this picture of the traditional community will have a strong appeal, for it seems to confirm our vision of our more distant European past and to reinforce what Romantic art and literature, and even household legends and fairytales, have told us about a way of life that was simpler and in many respects more intimate. But is that not largely because we are seeing it from the perspective of more than two hundred years of radical change? In actuality that traditional inhabited landscape achieved a coherent form only after generations of unrest and confusion. Almost by definition an inhabited landscape is the product of incessant adaptation and conflict: adaptation to what is often a new and bewildering natural environment, conflict between groups of people with very dissimilar views as to how to make that adaptation. The political landscape, artificial though it may be, is the realization of an archetype, of a coherent design inspired by philosophy or religion, and it has a distinct purpose in view. But the inhabited landscape is, to use a much distorted word, an existential landscape: it achieves its identity only in the course of existence. Only when it ceases to evolve can we say what it is.

Tönnies was, of course, chiefly interested in the final form of the traditional community and its landscape. He has nothing to say about the repeated confrontations, environmental as well as social, that took place from the very first moment of settlement. Nevertheless those were part of the story of the landscape, and we can see their scars even now; for if the landscape is often divided and analyzed into natural or topographical spaces—and the tendency to do this is becoming stronger—instead of into political or "civic" spaces, that is because the landscape is now interpreted as a way of adapting to the natural order.

Speaking of land ownership in the earliest Germanic communities, Jacob Grimm observes that the population

lives by raising livestock and by farming. . . . Now it is obvious that for the herder land which is undivided and under group control is desirable, while the farmer prefers individual control. The herder needs established pastureland, meadows and forest for grazing and mast; his livestock thrive only by being held together in one place. To the farmer the best piece of land is the one surrounding his homestead that he can fence and from which he can exclude all outsiders. He plows the land by himself and the prosperity of his farm depends solely on his own efforts. . . . Thus we see divided property and property operated jointly side by side, the undivided, collectively exploited holding being the older and the obsolescent.[28]

So the original landscape which the settlers take over is seen as a composition of *natural* spaces, some suited to farming, some suited to grazing, others covered with wood and brush, but all of them, when seen together, suited to communal exploitation. None of the spaces is actually unchangeable as to size or shape. Flexible boundaries are a hallmark of the inhabited landscape, for as the community grows, as its economy shifts from stock-raising to farming or vice versa, or one or another of the spaces decreases in value, then a shift, a gradual spatial reorganization ensues. But essentially these are the spaces those early migrants or settlers always looked for: land for grazing and land for farming. In fact they had *four* spaces in mind: for the site of the village, for arable, for livestock, and finally forest; but forest was omnipresent and in any case it was valued more for its grass than for its wood. As for the village site, that was understood. This is why, throughout the centuries of European history, we hear of the need for two spaces: deeds and leases and petitions for land for settlement mention them in English or French or Latin or German.

Labourage et *paturage, ager* and *saltus, Allmende* [the woods and wasteland open to collective exploitation by the village community] and *Gewannen* [the areas of cultivation]. . . . The combination seems in effect to be constant and fundamental throughout the Middle Ages. Three concentric zones, so to speak, the enclosed village, the space devoted to raising grain, and finally the large belt left uncultivated; such was the image of the village of his childhood kept by the author of the *Annales Cameracenses* toward the end of the 12th century. Three zones where the human presence thins out as it moves from the inhabited center, but three zones equally useful, equally sustaining.[29]

For many centuries the tripartite division of the landscape remained a reality. In the seventeenth century, when Englishmen arrived in New England they organized their towns or villages in strict accordance with the old system. Each qualified inhabitant of a new settlement was granted, in addition to a home lot in the village itself, a portion of meadow, a portion of land for tillage, and a woodlot. And although the prompt decay of the traditional open field system in the colony and the development of private farms independently operated put an end to the search for village self-sufficiency, the belief that every farm should automatically contain meadow, field, and woodland remained as strong as ever. *The New England Farmer or Georgical Dictionary,* compiled in 1797, recommended that "lots designed chiefly for tillage should be nearest to the house and barn . . . the mowing lots for pasturage should be contrived to be next, and the woodlots furthest of all lots from the house." The reason offered for each location was convenience and the saving of labor. Even so, the old medieval hierarchy of spaces, the system of three concentric zones was still discernable.

By the beginning of the twentieth century the almost total reorganization of the American farm, its increasing mechanization, its emphasis on one commercial crop, and the declining usefulness of the woodlot opened the eyes of most farmers to the impracticability of the old three-part division.

We have now devised entirely new ways of classifying land—an indication, I think, that we have gone a long way toward formulating a new definition of the landscape itself.

The Forest, Its Rise and Fall

In the traditional medieval concept of the universe the whole world was likewise divided into three spaces: one was where men lived and where they created their own defined spaces—gardens and plowed fields. A second was the open space where cattle grazed and where there were no fences, and a third space was everything beyond. In Latin these were called, respectively, *ager, saltus,* and *silva:* "horrida silva," according to Tacitus. In English they were village and arable (or landscape in the strict sense of the word), grazing or common or wasteland (including woodland), and then wilderness.

Forest is a relatively new word, and we ought not use it at this juncture, for we are attempting to see the world as the peasant of the Dark Ages saw it. Where *we* see a familiar and beautiful element, the forest, *he* saw wilderness. *Wood* and *weald* and *wald* all derive from *wild,* meaning lawless and unpredictable. Even so, we cannot always be sure of how in those times the word was being used. Sometimes *wood* signified a forest mountain range, as with the Böhmerwald in Germany. Sometimes it signified a boundary, a protective zone. But the original basic meaning of *wood* usually prevailed: wilderness or even desert. If we turn to Latin we find (as we might expect) a greater variety of words for wooded areas with specialized functions, but still no word for a forest. *Silva* (from which we get *savage*) usually indicated wilderness or primeval forest—definitely not part of the human landscape. *Nemus* was a park or an artificial plantation, a *lucas* was a sacred grove. *Saltus* in medieval charters meant woodland with grazing. It seems originally to have indicated a mountain pass, and since Romans associated such passes with forested mountains, the word meant *both* forest and frontier. Eventually, however, *saltus* came to mean a pasture where there were trees, something like an open range.

In legendary times in northern Europe the great mass of the wilderness (or forest), the seemingly endless reaches of trees and vegetation and inaccessible mountainsides and valleys remained untouched. It was seen, two thousand and more years ago, simply as wilderness; a vast, featureless, inhospitable region not unlike the open sea in its terrors. "The absence of large-scale clearing cannot simply be explained by the technical incompetence of the Germans," an historian remarks.

> They valued the primeval forest: it was impassable and untouchable. There were great frontier stretches of forest between the tribes. The heart of the forest was the seat of the Godhead; there it displayed its awe; there it claimed sacrifice and humble submission. . . . We cannot say that this numinous atmosphere absolutely forbade the pushing of settlement into the woods. But it was a hindrance, and is at least evidence that the Germans looked on the woodland in whose midst they dwelt as an unchangeable thing.[30]

Still, there was clearly a distinction made, even in the remotest times, between the heart of the primeval forest, what could be termed the "heroic" forest associated with myth and mythic divinities, and the everyday or folk forest which each community needed in its tripartite landscape. And for this relatively insignificant part of the forest there existed a name. *March* is a word now little used; it refers to a border area or boundary. In Gothic times it seems to have meant *both* boundary and forest, and it is easy to understand how this could have been the case. When communities were little more than oases in the midst of the northern wilderness, the edge of the surrounding

Farm surrounded by forest, near Spokane. (U.S.D.A., Soil Conservation Service)

forest was identified with the community frontier; seen as a landmark, a feature of some sanctity, not to be violated, so the original meaning of *march* or *mark* was forest, and specifically the edge of the forest where the trees had been thinned out and where the cattle grazed. The word is clearly related to *margin* and *merge*—and even *murky*.

Here a different terminology can help us. If we see the forest as a distinct ecological entity we then define that margin as a degraded forest environment, an example of mismanagement and abuse. But if, instead of that, we see the forest simply as wilderness, then the margin clearly does not belong in it. It becomes *saltus,* grazing land; *march,* a word meaning both woodland and frontier, an essential space since it contained an abundance of resources: herbs, wild fruit, game, raw materials for many crafts, wood for fuel and for building, and above all, stands of grass. "Forests also hath Britain," Geoffrey of Monmouth wrote in the twelfth century, "filled with every manner of wild deer, in the glades whereof groweth grass that the cattle may find therein change of pasture." At a period when cultivated grasses were unknown and grasses of any sort had to compete with weeds, these grassgrown glades—or lawns as they were called—were much prized. Yet most of the feed for the livestock consisted of branches of foliage cut from the forest trees—a practice which had the effect of making the forest margin even more open.

Only a southern farmer can really understand the concept of woodland as grazing land. To this day we can observe in the rural parts of the South cows and hogs and even horses wandering and grazing at will in what used to be called waste: abandoned fields, cut-over woods, the margins of roads and highways, much as animals did in northern Europe more than a thousand years ago. The custom is one of the last reminders in America of a time when forest (or wilderness) was not a part of that composition of defined spaces known as a landscape, when the very word *forest* was all but unknown to the average Englishman. It came into existence in courtly circles in the ninth century to identify a part of the wilderness set aside for the king's hunting. The word, H. C. Darby informs us, "is neither a botanical nor a geographical term, but a legal term. It implied land *outside* (foris) the common law and subject to a special law that safeguarded the king's hunting. Forest and woodland were thus not synonymous terms, for the forested areas included land that was neither wood or waste, and they sometimes included whole counties. Even so, a forested area usually contained some wood and often large tracts of wood."[31]

However restrictive its original meaning might have been, the invention of this word marks one of the first steps in what can be called the discovery or the creation of the forest as a distinct ecological entity. For then it began to be seen as part of the life—social, economic, ecological, and spiritual—of every Atlantic landscape. The history of this discovery is a separate and as yet unwritten chapter in landscape studies. It starts with the legal definition, more than a millennium ago, of the forest as a *political* space, a space with its own special law. At an early date three—even four—kinds of forests were created, each with its own special legal status: the royal forest, the chase, the park, and the warren. The clearly defined forest, the forest as a visible element in the rural countryside distinct from open farmland, probably dates from the sixteenth century; according to a forest historian, "A firm boundary between forest and field did not exist before the 14th century. Men set fire to parts of the forest whenever it was convenient, planted grain for a year or two, and when the soil no longer produced a crop, abandoned the clearing, and the woods grew back again."[32]

Perhaps it is premature to lament the passing of the old-fashioned multi-purpose forest, small, mismanaged, and open to everyone: hunters, botanists, woodcutters, poetic searchers after *Waldeinsamkeit* (the solitude of the forest), stray cows. Yet it sometimes seems as if it were being replaced by a multitude of scientifically organized special purpose forests: commercial forests of a single kind of tree, forests for public recreation with informative signs on the trees, forests for watershed management, flood control, forests as model ecosystems, forests as sound barriers, forests as works of art, but no more forest as such. And when that happens the word itself will be abandoned as lacking in precision, and we will be back once more to the medieval wood-land margin; only it will be the margin of the highway.

Mobility and Immobility

Despite our strong emotional attachment to these inhabited landscapes and what they once meant to us, it is far from easy to grasp their essential characteristics, and when it is a matter of interpreting them in terms of space, I confess I am often at a loss. But the shifting status of the forest can perhaps provide a clue, for it long played a dominant role in our landscape history.

Geographically speaking, that role has been thoroughly investigated. We have learned through a variety of archeological techniques how and when and where the forests covering much of Atlantic Europe were fragmented, reduced in extent, and how their exploitation became increasingly efficient and destructive. What we know much less about is the manner in which our perception, our definition of the forest has changed over the centuries, and how we discovered and explored the forest and its resources and finally integrated it in the man-made landscape.

How are we to chronicle that intellectual process? It is much as if, in prehistoric times, a mist, a primeval cloud of the unknowing had slowly started to dissipate, revealing first of all the limitless and terrifying atmo-sphere of wildness surrounding the inhabited world, then the more clearly defined *space,* the wilderness composed of wooded mountains, a frontier protection against chaos. Finally comes the exploitation of the woodland margin, a zone where livestock were grazed and wood for building and burning was collected. In the twelfth century there are signs that the wilderness is being defined no longer as frontier, as march, but as part of the village territory, which gradually expands as the marginal woodland is eroded. It was perhaps some three centuries later that villagers and others learned to see the wilderness from a new perspective, borrowed the word *forest,* established boundaries, and (in short) tamed and humanized this tree-grown space, so that it became a fraction of the village landscape, essentially no different in status from the field or the common.

But the stage that interests us is that in which the forest is first perceived as a natural space used in common by all members of the village. The forest or woodland belongs to everyone. "Property in land begins with possession in common," Grimm observes; "the forest in which I picked an apple, the meadow where I graze my cattle, belongs to *us.* The land which we defend against enemies, belongs to *us;* soil and earth, the air in which we live—no one can own even a fragment of these for himself. They are owned in common; like fire and water they belong to all."

Thus the distinct natural spaces—meadow, moor, forest, etc., as well as the four elements—can never be permanently divided into individual holdings. Specifically, no individual using them can build a fence around any portion of them. In fact the only permanent walls or fences in the inhabited landscape are those surrounding an area sanctified by myth: the site of the original homesteads, the village itself as a built-up area, the communal fields, and the meadow. Within the forest (as it begins to be exploited) only temporary fences, such as those around grazing areas or a stand of valuable trees, are allowed. The locations of permanent boundaries are established by means of what seem to us to be haphazard procedures—the throwing of a hammer, the flight of a chicken, the distance a sound could carry, etc.—intended to symbolize their divine, inscrutable nature. When walls or fences are not practicable, as in the boundaries of a whole community, then stone markers or certain long-lived trees are planted.

This sort of boundary—religious and unchangeable in character, periodically verified and solemnly rededicated—is very much what we saw in the political landscape, and insofar as it is intended to define a permanent space—village or commons—it has its political aspect here. But within this more or less rigid network of boundaries there exists a vast number of smaller spaces constantly shifting in shape and size. These are the plots of ground farmed by the villagers, the short-term enclosures in the forest or the meadow; and even the pieces of land occupied by the more modest houses—altogether comprising much the greater part of the village and arable. We are thus in that part of the inhabited landscape where change and mobility are the rule.

In the medieval European landscape—and briefly in the seventeenth-century landscape of New England—these farmed plots were assembled in two, sometimes three, large fields called open fields because none of those plots was fenced, even though the fields themselves were. The field is one of the most elusive spaces in the landscape and requires some definition, for it differs in meaning in every landscape period.

Now commonly defined as "a cultivated open expanse of land, usually devoted to one crop," it was a *natural* space in the inhabited landscape, like forest or moor. The word derives from an Indo-European root, *pele,* meaning a flat, open space, as can be seen in related words like *plain, palm* of the hand, and *Poland.* Even in the early Middle Ages *feld* meant "land free from wood, lying on downs and moors, or sometimes in the open spaces of the forest."[33]

As a *natural* space it was therefore *community* property and was surrounded by a fence or hedge. It was, as I say, divided into sometimes hundreds of individual parcels, used (but not owned) by the various households in the village. Though they were of different shapes and sizes they were hard to distinguish one from another, for in every field the same crops were grown, and none of them contained any tree or perennial plant, or any structure, nor were there any roads, any communal spaces or installations in the fields to serve the innumerable parcels of land: a strictly utilitarian uniform collection of spaces.

But for several understandable reasons this pattern of parcels within each field underwent constant change: sometimes because of divisions brought about by inheritance, sometimes by consolidation, sometimes because of a gradual shift in boundary as a neighbor surreptitiously plowed one more furrow. After a few generations there was often such distortion and confusion that a drastic reorganization of the spaces was called for. Since most of these changes were unrecorded, and the land transactions among the tenants were verbal, never documented, scholars have found it all but impossible to chronicle them, much less interpret them, and in any case there were economic and technological reasons for the mobility. Writing about the Continental landscape in the very early Middle Ages, Marc Bloch says:

> The arable land from which the village derived its sustenance was necessarily much larger in proportion to the number of inhabitants than it is today. For agriculture was a great devourer of space. In the tilled fields, incompletely plowed and almost always inadequately manured, the ears of [wheat] grew neither very heavy nor very dense. Above all, the harvests never covered the whole area of cultivation at once. The most advanced systems of crop-rotation known to the age required that every year half or a third of the cultivated soil should lie fallow. Often indeed, fallow and crops followed each other in irregular alternation, which always allowed more time for the growth of weeds than for that of the cultivated produce; the fields, in such cases, represented hardly more than a provisional and short-lived conquest of the wasteland, and even in the heart of agricultural regions nature tended constantly to regain the upper hand. Beyond them, enveloping them, thrusting into them, spread

forest, scrub and dunes—immense wilderness, seldom entirely uninhabited by man, though whoever dwelt there as a charcoal-burner, shepherd, hermit or outlaw did so only at the cost of a long separation from his fellow men.[34]

Nor was this spatial fluidity confined to the open fields. Most of the roads—strictly speaking "rights of way"—in the inhabited landscape were temporary spaces designed for temporary use. Village authorities would designate a strip of land for the hauling of wood from the forest or for driving cattle to the village. Once these tasks were accomplished the road ceased to have any legal existence.

Braudel mentions the "relative mobility of villages and hamlets" in the later Middle Ages. "They grew up, expanded, contracted, and also shifted their sites. Sometimes these 'desertions' were total and final. . . . More often the center of gravity within a given cultural area shifted, and everything—furniture, people, animals, stones—was moved out of the abandoned village to a site a few kilometers away. Even the form of the village could change in the course of these vicissitudes."[35]

In ancient Germanic law, the house or cottage counted as movable goods. The term also included a great variety of things: livestock, household goods, weapons, bees, and even certain vegetable products. Thus in some landscapes mobile property included grass (and crops) moved by the wind and branches blown down from trees. Grimm tells us that in a certain part of Germany fruit growing in the country was considered immobile, whereas buildings, hedges, fences, and implements were considered movable; on the other hand masonry walls and anything built with nails were considered attached to the earth and immovable. One of the complications in studying the inhabited landscape is that each region, each village is likely to have its own unwritten laws and customs, and such unwritten laws and customs will vary over time and apply to one class in the population and not to another. Generally speaking, mobile property was the only possession of women, minors, and those of the lowest social status; only free men (however defined) were entitled to own land—presumably inherited from a remote legendary ancestor. The average peasant could only *use* land belonging to others, and then only the surface, to raise a movable crop or graze his mobile livestock. Ancient Greece made a similar distinction in kinds of ownership, but it was not between mobile and immobile; it was between invisible and visible—visible signifying what was permanent.

Nature, Tame and Wild

In another of his composite period landscapes Ruskin describes the landscape of the Middle Ages as depicted in medieval art. But we are given few details of the everyday, "mobile" world, for the perspective is that of the nobleman, and the medieval nobleman, unlike his peers in Classical antiquity, had no taste for work or the place of work; above all no taste or tolerance for the workers themselves. Viewed, therefore, from the castle heights,

> the pleasant flatland is never a ploughed field, nor a rich lotus meadow good for pasture, but *garden* ground covered with flowers, and divided by fragrant hedges, with a castle in the middle of it. The aspens are delighted in, not because they are good for "coach-making men" to make cart-wheels of, but because they are shady and graceful; and the fruit trees, covered with delicious fruit, especially apple and orange, occupy still more important positions in the scenery. . . . And the ideal occupation of mankind is not to cultivate either the garden or the meadow, but to gather roses and eat oranges in the one, and ride out hawking over the other.[36]

Ruskin summarizes the aristocratic feeling toward nature: "Love of the garden instead of love of the farm. . . . Loss of sense of actual Divine presence, leading to fancies of fallacious animation, in herbs, flowers, etc. perpetual and more or less undisturbed companionship with wild nature."

Much depends, I would say, on how wild the nature was. We have a good example of an inhabited landscape in the American Southwest, where the Pueblo Indians have established and maintained over the centuries a very satisfactory companionship with the environment. But that is because both parties display the same measure and predictability and willingness to cooperate. The complexity of the Southwest is strictly geological: in terms of habitability it is simplicity itself: there has to be water and sun, there has to be a dependable calendar, and there has to be space. The Pueblo people are partial to clear-cut distinctions in society, in time, and in space, and as a result they have created a very efficient inhabited landscape. "The Zuni Indians," said Ruth Benedict,

> do not picture the universe, as we do, as a conflict of good and evil. They are not dualistic. . . . It is difficult for us to lay aside our picture of the universe as a struggle between good and evil and see it as the Pueblos see it. They do not see the seasons, nor man's life, as a race run by life and death. . . . The seasons unroll. Life is always present, death is always present . . . like their version of man's relation to other men, their versions of man's relation to the cosmos gives no place to heroism and man's will to overcome obstacles. . . . They have made, in one small but long-established cultural island in North America, a civilization whose forms are dictated by the typical choices of the Apollonian, all of whose delight is in formality and whose way of life is the way of measure and sobriety.[37]

This could never be said of the medieval landscape of northern Europe—an inhabited landscape like that of the Pueblo Indians insofar as it was the expression of a desire to come to terms with its environment. No doubt the medieval inhabitants were different to start with, but we cannot ignore the quality of the environment they confronted: the long, dark winters making for solitude and introspection, the sudden liberating spring when all living things are growing and moving and starting afresh. And of course there is the omnipresent forest, the place of myth and death and freedom; somehow or other it has to be dealt with, and a sense of uncertainty, totally absent from the Pueblo relationship, enters the picture, a sense that "history" will eventually take over. The giants which haunt the forest are bitterly resentful of man's presence and take particular pains to destroy church belfries—symbols of a new faith and of an ordering of time, and even elves, much more numerous, much more friendly, and often very helpful, lament the disappearance of the forest and the spread of farming. Their cry, "Our king is dead," is sometimes heard in the remoter woodlands. If any superstition could be said to epitomize that early and transient relationship between an illiterate society and its environment it would be the widespread belief in the existence of the Little People. Any firmly held belief in the invisible, it seems to me, must somehow affect our attitude toward the *visible* world, and what might have been little more than a random plundering and destruction of the nearby wilderness became an exchange of benefits: those things which men took from the forest for their daily needs were repaid by our helping and protecting and loving the small, invisible creatures who lived there. They served as intermediaries, they reassured us that we were taking part in the natural order and were not entirely alien to it.

Despite their small size—the true elf is never taller than a four-year-old child (but then that was the height ascribed by the Middle Ages to angels as well)—elves had many affinities with man, and because of all creatures only they and man were created directly by God, they dream of being admitted to heaven. "Through the whole existence of elves, nixes and goblins," Grimm writes,

> there runs a low undercurrent of the unsatisfied, disconsolate: they do not rightly know how to turn their glorious gifts to account, they always require to lean upon man . . . though acquainted in a higher degree than men with the hidden virtues of stones and herbs, they yet evoke human aid for their sick and their women in labor, they borrow men's vessels for baking and brewing, they even celebrate their weddings and high times in the halls of men. Hence too their doubting whether they can be partakers of salvation, and their unconcealed grief when a negative answer is given.[38]

Habitat and Habit

This close, never-ceasing relationship with the environment is typical of every inhabited landscape, whether it is Pueblo or northern European or African, but we need to remind ourselves that the relationship is confined to *one* particular environment, which means that all other environments no matter

how similar (as in the case of the Pueblo Indians) are excluded—and so are
their inhabitants. The political landscape is indifferent to the topography and
culture of the territories it takes over, but the inhabited landscape sees itself as
the center of the world, an oasis of order in the surrounding chaos, inhabited
by the People. Insularity is what gives it character; size, wealth, beauty have
nothing to do with it; it is a law unto itself.

Actually not a law, but a set of habits and customs accumulated over the
centuries, each the outcome of a slow adaptation to place—to the local
topography and weather and soil, and to the people, the superfamily which
lived there: a special accent, a special way of dressing, a special form of
greeting; special dances and holidays—all the picturesque idiosyncracies that
are the stuff of tourist folklore, and then some: passwords and gestures,
taboos and secrets—secret places and secret events that exclude the outsider
more effectively than any boundary. Strange how many of these customs,
these ways of identifying an inhabited landscape and its inhabitants are senso-
ry: the unmistakable taste of a local dish or a local wine, the smell of certain
seasons, the sound of a local song! There was a time when the territory of
many villages was the countryside where the churchbell could be heard—like
the old-fashioned definition of a Cockney: someone born within sound of
Bowbells. Sensations such as these are never entirely forgotten; not that they
are much thought about, but they remind us that we are where we belong—
and equally important, I think: they are not shared with outsiders.

Is that what we mean by a sense of place? Is this total adjustment to and
immersion in the inhabited landscape what we aspire to? I hope not, for at
their most beautiful and rewarding, our European–American landscapes
stand for a very different relationship. Explain it how we will—religious
insight, psychological shift, growing awareness of the wider world outside
the village, or whatever—there came a time some five centuries ago when we
began to see the landscape from a new and more detached perspective. The
villager in the old inhabited landscape was never an efficient farmer nor
interested in changing his ways. He had not presumed to inquire into the
hidden aspects of nature: the composition of the soil, the development of
plants, the vagaries of the weather; all that he knew was what his senses told
him. But then he discovered that he had a distinct, human role to play. "The
farmer," says an ancient handbook of agriculture, "should study the nature of
the land from which he expects to make a living, and diligently learn whether
the soil is cold or warm, moist or dry, sandy or clayey. . . . For just as every
man and every animal has his own peculiarities, every field has its own
nature." He was further urged to treat the land as a teacher treats a child
whom he wants to develop into a responsible individual, or think of himself
as a midwife, helping bring something into the world. He was to see himself
as a trainer who patiently encourages the best and most useful traits in a colt
or a young dog. In short, he was no longer to be a drudge, blindly following

routines from the past, he was to be a guardian, a teacher, a helper. In the old sense of the word, the farmer undertook to *improve* his land, to bring it to its natural perfection, and this required of him that he learn to recognize the *invisible* potential of soils and animals and plants, the landscape of universal law instead of the landscape of local custom.

Connecticut River Valley in South Deerfield, Massachusetts. (Photo: Gordon Parks)

The Connecticut River Valley is a man-made landscape of exceptional age and beauty. It is one of the classic historic landscapes of the United States. To our generation its towns and villages and farmlands epitomize New England of the eighteenth and early nineteenth centuries. To those who first explored it, almost 350 years ago, the valley offered the first reassuring glimpse of the rich New World they had dreamt of but had failed to find on the shores of Massachusetts Bay. Sixteen years after the landing at Plymouth, settlers had found their way west, and they came in increasing numbers throughout the seventeenth century.

Despite Indian raids and wars, the settlements multiplied and prospered, and as the meadows and areas of cultivation grew closer together the valley became something more than a topographical concept. It became a landscape, perhaps the most extensive and certainly the most clearly defined human landscape in New England.

Throughout the eighteenth century, travelers going by stagecoach between Boston and the Hudson River towns must have welcomed the sight of the fields and the scattering of villages in the valley—doubly welcome after the rough, forested stretches of Massachusetts or the hills of western Connecticut. In their letters home or in their published accounts they often described the pattern of settlement, the abundance of sheep and cattle, and the prosperous farms.

The best and most detailed eighteenth-century description was written by Timothy Dwight in 1796. He had shortly before been chosen president of Yale and had decided to devote his summer vacations to exploring New York State and New England. For the next ten years he did so, and the four volumes of his *Travels,* recently reissued by the Harvard University Press, constitute one of the most valuable accounts of the American landscape and its settlement that we have.

Dwight, as a theologian, preacher, and educator, was firmly loyal to the Puritan tradition and also an ardent defender of all things American. The two convictions produced an extremely fresh and opinionated appraisal of the environment: although he detested the crude lawlessness of frontier society as he saw it in upper New York State, he had an insatiable interest in every unknown or unexplored aspect of the American landscape and a quick appreciation of scenic beauty, no matter how untamed. The Connecticut Valley, with its vivid memories of Dwight's grandfather, Jonathan Edwards, and with the splendor of its mountains, delighted him; he expressed his approval in long passages of stately prose.

The section describing the view over the Connecticut Valley from the summit of Mount Holyoke is far too long to quote in full. Dwight starts with the broad river meandering between its tree-grown banks; he then gives a picture of the fields, meadows, and roads, where

a perfect neatness and brilliancy is everywhere diffused, without a neglected spot to
tarnish the luster or excite a wish in the mind for a higher finish. When [the eye]
marks the sprightly towns which rise upon [the river's] banks, and the numerous
churches which gem the whole landscape in its neighborhood; when it explores the
lofty forests, wildly contrasted with the rich scene of cultivation . . . and when last
of all it fastens upon the Monadnock in the northeast and in the northwest upon
Saddle Mountain, ascending each at a distance of fifty miles in dim and misty
grandeur, far above all other objects of view; it will be difficult not to say that with
these exquisite varieties of beauty and grandeur the relish for landscape is filled,
neither a wish for a higher perfection, nor an idea of what it is remaining in the
mind.

At least two aspects of this passage are worthy of note. First, in its complete, unedited form it constitutes a single sentence, suspended from various
semicolons, of more than 250 words. Second, from the pen of an eighteenth-
century New England theologian has come one of the clearest and most
eloquent statements of the Protestant point of view toward the environment
and the man-made landscape. It is sometimes said that because of his unusual
awareness of natural beauty Dwight was the first of America's nature roman-
tics. But there is no trace of romanticism in his unemotional description of
the beauty confronting him; there is no melancholy yearning for more, no
despairing self-deprecation. "The relish for landscape," he says, "is filled."
And he presumably withdrew from Mount Holyoke, his identity intact.

What was the nature of the scenic beauty that Dwight sought to describe?
What were to him the significant landscape values? I think we can say that
they were essentially religious. Twice in that one passage he expresses an
awareness of having glimpsed completeness, of having glimpsed the highest
form of perfection, and the emphasis on "the perfect neatness and brilliancy"
of the scene, its jewel-like aspect, reminds us of that mystic vision which
Aldous Huxley analyzed in *The Doors of Perception*. We could no doubt dismiss that phrase concerning "the idea" of a higher perfection as rhetoric,
were it not that the focus of the entire panorama (as Dwight viewed it) was
the village in the valley directly below. Here was the heart of the landscape: a
pattern of fields, orchards, and houses, with the church in the center, all
surrounded by the protective wall of forest and mountain. To the Calvinist
theologian the village was little less than the symbol of piety, community, and
mutual love, of "pure religion breathing household laws." The landscape, in
short, possessed the quality of beauty insofar as it reflected the moral or
ethical perfection to which all its inhabitants presumably aspired. Perfection
or completeness resided not in the landscape itself, but in the spirit that had
brought it into being and continued to animate it. This spirit was the Puritan
spirit, that of a population devoted, in Dwight's words, "to the worship of
Jehovah." Not every landscape possessed these qualities; Dwight was critical
of other types of settlement. He condemned the backwoods communities of

the New York or Vermont wilderness because they had no such religious origin. To Dwight and his contemporaries a landscape was beautiful only when it revealed or confirmed a moral or ethical truth.

This kind of appraisal is not one we in our generation are likely to find congenial, but it had merits. The man-made landscape that he found worthy of praise was certainly not lavish or varied; it did not change or expand with grace; it was suited to a meager way of life. But Dwight's humanism never disdained the commonplace, never exalted the exotic and wonderful at the expense of everyday necessity. It never sought to wean men from society or to foster a fruitless nostalgia for the primitive. However devoid such humanism may have been of a feeling for the picturesque, it never created landscapes that were lonely; it endowed everyone who lived and worked in them with a kind of visibility, an identity tied to a fragment of the land itself. At all events this landscape, nowhere more extensive than in the Connecticut Valley, was in those early days of the republic the best we had. The Puritan village, stripped of its churchly characteristics, was the inspiration for the new rectangular landscape that came into existence west of the Alleghenies with the Land Ordinance of 1785. It was the eighteenth-century New England community, inhabited and self-governed by a small society of independent farmers, that Jefferson and others sought in fact to reproduce when they devised the range and township and section system which still prevails over most of the United States.

As we know, that particular agrarian dream failed to become a reality. But it took several decades to die, and I think we can say that it survived, although in an attenuated form, until after the Civil War. What eventually replaced the moral–ethical perception of the landscape was the vision of the engineer. We are only now beginning to study the origins and growth of the engineer's landscape and the insidious manner in which the engineer's philosophy has affected our attitudes toward every landscape, even while we denounce it.

In his earliest guise, the engineer in America seemed to be exclusively devoted to the community—even the Puritan community. Toward the end of his life Dwight noted with approval the construction of dams and canals throughout New England; at the same time Albert Gallatin, likewise a defender of the humanist tradition, launched a national program of internal improvements. Although many of these improvements were designed to serve the rising commercial and manufacturing interests, Dwight and his contemporaries managed to discover their moral justification; they not only created wealth, they discouraged idleness and taught skills. Forts, harbors, bridges, and roads, designed by engineers, were interpreted as signs of concern for the community and its welfare. It was not long after Dwight's death that the engineer further adorned the landscape by the building of railroads. But even this modification of the environment retained, visually at least, something of that civic quality suggested in the term *civil engineer*. For it was he who built the massive viaducts and bridges, who provided the rural as well as the urban landscape of America with a kind of granite infrastructure that still impresses us by its monumentality.

Only in the 1860s did the engineer begin to discard his civil allegiance, and that took place when he entered the employ of industry. His new clients, rich and ambitious, transformed him into the single most powerful environmental force in America, although a force entirely under their control. With the rise of the steam-powered factory, the multiplication of railroads, and the search for new natural resources, the concern of the engineer ceased to be civic or national and concentrated instead on the production, conservation, and use of energy—energy from water, coal, gas, and wood, energy in the form of steam and electricity, and ultimately in the form of human labor. Inevitably, the American landscape reflected his efforts: not only in the rail lines, coal mines, hydroelectric dams, oil wells, and the multitude of factories and company towns; even the contemporary superhighway expresses the engineer's skill in conveying energy from one side of the nation to the other. And it cannot be forgotten that it was the engineer's obsession with plentiful and reliable energy that largely inspired the conservation movement of seventy years ago, as well as our own contemporary manner of interpreting economic difficulties.

Thus we are confronted with another implicit definition of environmental values: to the engineer (and to the engineer-minded society) a landscape is beautiful when the energy-flow system is functioning with unimpeded efficiency. Is it necessary to point out how similar this view is to the concept of the average ecologist?

For it was not simply the environment that the engineer modified; the whole temper of American life and thought was changed, and permanently changed. By the end of the nineteenth century the majority of Americans were already living in towns and cities; the majority of Americans, that is, had pretty well broken their ties with the rural landscape and had begun to forget the role that the landscape had once played in the formation of their character and identity. I do not mean to imply that the new industrial order invariably meant a lowering of the quality of the environment of the average American. Quite the contrary: many small farmers and farm laborers were happy to exchange their exhausted acres and squalid houses for less strenuous work in a factory and a home in a company town. Nevertheless, the old covenant had been broken or annulled; there were no longer any agrarian routines and duties to teach citizenship and piety; without attachment to some piece of land, men lost one kind of visibility. And how were the values of the landscape to be perceived when they no longer taught a lesson? Furthermore, the urban American found that all significant experiences, good or bad, now usually took place in the company of many other people, often strangers, and in environments owned or controlled either by the public authority or by a corporation: factory, office, or store; beach, park, or sports arena—environments for which the average citizen did not and could not feel any responsibility.

We are prone to exaggerate the consequences of this alienation and loss of visibility. It is hard for us to admit that most human qualities, like hydroponic vegetables, manage to flourish even when they have no roots in the soil. But there can be no doubt that an entirely new relationship to the environment has evolved over the past century of engineer control, or rather two distinct relationships.

One, with which literature has made us very familiar, is the indignant rejection of the engineer's world, with its dirt, confusion, and crowds, and flight to the wilderness. The other reaction, far more general and far less articulate, and on that account generally ignored by students of environmental perception, was acceptance of the situation, a readiness to take whatever pleasures were made available in an increasingly urbanized environment. A lingering romantic tradition, popular in the academic and upper-class world, finds little of value in that acceptance and laments the crowded holiday highways, the crowded ball parks, the crowded beaches, the meretricious forms of recreation. But what some of us call crowds, others call people, and many enjoy these pastimes not as surrogates for the vanished agrarian experience, but as something entirely new and rewarding.

In any case, whether we abandon the engineered landscape in favor of the wilderness or whether we embrace it, we are expressing an identical attitude toward the environment; and that attitude is essentially that of the engineer. The landscape is no longer the locus of character formation, for carrying out traditional obligations; it is now a place where certain resources can be bought or had for free. Our objective is that of the engineer: to accumulate energy, whether psychic or physical, and then to transfer it to the city.

Finally, one more characteristic of the contemporary evaluation of the natural environment, although obvious enough, should not be omitted, because it too is the product of the engineer way of life. Our contacts with that environment are not only brief and infrequent, but scheduled, taking place on holidays and weekends, determined not by seasons but by the routine of urban work. So these contacts are events to be looked forward to, planned, and long remembered. The natural environment thus becomes the setting of an experience, rather than the experience itself.

What is the nature of that experience? How does it differ from the traditional experience of the wilderness explorer? In three specific ways: the contemporary experience is not solitary, it is not contemplative, and it is less concerned with awareness of the environment as a distinct phenomenon than it is with the cultivation of self-awareness.

This is not the place to expatiate on this new search for self-awareness by means of new sports or skills of mobility and intimate contact with the less

familiar aspects of the environment: wind, slope, surface texture, depths of
water, aerial heights; they represent, I think, a potentially valuable search for
identity by means of a new kind of environmental experience, and quite
clearly they call for new kinds of environment, part natural, part engineered.
Such activities are distinctly urban insofar as they do not reject the presence
of others. And insofar as this search for self-awareness has its religious or
mystical quality, it is important to bear in mind that solitude is not a necessary or even a desirable ingredient. Here again we are often the victims of a
romantic tradition which has insisted that religious insight comes only to the
solitary seeker. But the thousands who gathered on the shores of the Sea of
Galilee were not unique. We have only to recall the crowds who collected on
the Boston Common to hear George Whitefield preach, the thousands who
gathered in the frontier forest clearings for revivals, or for that matter the tens
of thousands who gathered at Woodstock or Watkins Glen to recognize that
the open-air environment can offer as genuine an experience to the crowd as
to the individual.

It follows that we must learn to provide places for this kind of experience.
It is almost as if we were reverting to the attitude of Timothy Dwight:
discovering landscape beauty chiefly in those environments where men and
women achieve a more complete sense of their own identity. But the identity
we are after is, of course, far removed from that of Dwight's hardworking,
pious farmer, and it calls for a very different setting; far more spacious, far
less domestic, far less detailed. It is for the environmental planner and designer to formulate these settings and to discover how and where they can be
artificially created. There is, even now, no lack of suggestive examples: the
freeway, the ski slope, the wide expanse of public lawn, the wide expanse of
water, landscapes of space and freedom and unpredictability. Environmental
art can improve and perfect them and devise new ones.

A third definition of landscape beauty therefore suggests itself: a landscape
is beautiful when it has been or can be the scene of a significant experience in
self-awareness and eventual self-knowledge.

Agrophilia, or the
Love of Horizontal Spaces

Main street in Utah town showing disuse of upper stories.

◄ *Abandoned mill in Fall River, Massachusetts. (Photo: Todd Webb)*

There are landscapes in America separated by hundreds of miles that resemble one another to a bewildering degree. Many American towns, even many American cities, are all but indistinguishable as to layout, morphology, and architecture. The lack of variety in much of our man-made environment is recognized by anyone who has traveled widely in this country. Many deplore it, try to escape it, and because they cannot, suppose that America is altogether lacking the kind of landscape beauty characteristic of older parts of the world.

I have not found this to be the case. It is true that I cannot always remember the difference between one small town and another; both will have a main street flanked by solid buildings of brick, both will contain block after block of freestanding frame houses, each with a lawn; there will be a cluster of elegant white grain elevators near the railroad tracks in both of them, and a stretch of highway bordered by drive-ins; the towns are indeed much alike. But they are alike for a good reason: they consciously conform to what is a distinctive American style. *Classical* is the word for it, I think; and rhythmic repetition (not to say occasional monotony) is a Classical trait, the consequence of devotion to clarity and order. But the style also possesses spaciousness and dignity; that is why I relish the similarity between the villages of New England, the similarity between wheatfields whether in Oklahoma or Oregon, or the stately repetitiousness of North Dakota shelterbelts: they illustrate on a vast and generous scale that "noble simplicity and quiet grandeur" which Winckelmann associated with Classical works of art, and which, I believe, is more often met with in the landscape of the New World than in that of the Old. Much as the Roman traveler found reassurance in the identical grid layouts, the almost identical forums of the new towns in the more remote provinces of the Empire, saw them as affirmations of *Romanitas,* the traveler in the United States finds evidence wherever he goes of a specifically national style of spatial organization. He may not care for it, he may prefer a greater variety, a romantic confusion; but he cannot fail to be impressed by it.

Since the classical American town is easy to understand, its interest is soon exhausted. There is little to be gained from walking the length of still another Maple Street, inspecting still another colonnaded courthouse, another bank with clock/thermometer and drive-in window. But I have found that overfamiliarity with the scene has compensations: it teaches sensitivity to change, a sharpened awareness of any deviation from the established style; and if the evidence I have garnered during many years of visiting small towns is of any value, it indicates that the American landscape, the manner, that is to say, in which we have organized our space, is undergoing a remarkable shift.

Change in itself is not out of the ordinary; every cultural landscape has evolved, sometimes violently, more often slowly, over the centuries. What differs here is that we are able to watch the transformation as it takes place; able to record it and even to understand some of its causes. Signs of abandoned or superseded spatial organizations surround us; every ruin, whether in Asia Minor or in the American Southwest, reveals a fragment of a rural or urban landscape which became obsolete. But how? Obsolescence is a conveniently vague concept; in what stages was the place deserted? Which forms were first found wanting, which were maintained until the very end? Not all ruins mean sudden disaster; many represent a long series of decisions, choices between alternatives that we have no inkling of. All cities, all landscapes sooner or later come to an end; that we know. What we do not always know is how or why.

There is something like a culture of environmental change, a pattern of day-by-day decisions worth exploring. We can begin in America; and it is easiest to begin with evidence that is commonplace and accessible.

Who has not noticed (to take an example) that in almost every American town the upper stories of the buildings flanking Main Street are being deserted? Each year I see a few more windows dark and uncared for, even obliterated by commercial facades. Despite all the activity on the street floor, the second and third and fourth floors of the older brick buildings are no longer in demand. Not many years ago they accommodated the offices of lawyers and dentists and doctors; dance studios and certified public accountants. Now the gold lettering has vanished from the windows, and even the street door leading to the stairs is blocked. Sooner or later the buildings themselves will be torn down, to be replaced by one-story buildings or parking lots.

Such changes are so widespread that we rarely ask why they took place; we know the answer: the law firm needed more room, the doctor moved to be nearer the hospital, the dance studio required more modern wiring. Explanations vary, but they all indicate that the building had become obsolete.

Obsolescence of a different kind accounts for the changes along the tracks. Here the massive warehouses stand vacant, and the factory is closed; only on the ground floor, where a small firm makes handbags, is there activity. Ask why the factory has closed and the answer is simple: no one now buys cast-iron cookstoves; or the plant has moved to a better location on the highway. Either answer implies that these work spaces have ceased to serve their original purpose; given sufficient time and neglect they will become ruins.

Two further examples of change drive home the same lesson. Away from the center of the classical American town there is a residential section of tree-lined streets with houses surrounded by wide verandas and lawns. I knew it when it was lived in by prosperous families, the most desirable part of town. More than half the houses have been transformed into apartments. A schoolteacher lives on one floor, a retired couple on another, three students in the attic. The landlady occupies the rooms in the basement. Flanking the great front door of oak are four or five letter boxes. The lawn suffers from neglect. The original owners have either died or moved to a more spacious suburb.

One last typical change: the open country starts abruptly where the street becomes a road, and that is where a farmstead faces onto broad fields, with a large frame barn standing near it. Used until recently for storing feed, for sheltering some of the livestock, for many kinds of work, it has an air of being abandoned or of serving as a part-time garage. The two tall silos flanking it threaten to collapse. But back of the barn is a complex of new cement block buildings—long and low, with gleaming metal roofs.

We do not need to be told the significance of this melancholy change, nor do we need further instances of spatial reorganization brought about by obsolescence. But here is a change of another sort: on the outskirts of the town, in the midst of fields, a housing development—what its promoters call a planned residential community—has recently come into being. A compact mass of some fifty all but identical dwellings, Meadowview Heights occupies a rigidly bounded portion of what a few years ago was a cornfield, entirely flat. The development is laid out along a series of curving roads leading to no particular destination. The houses, painted in bright colors, are still too new to have acquired individuality; they lack gardens and all but the slimmest of trees. Still, the development has a quality of its own: it is an orderly composition of clear-cut, well-defined forms, in no way blending into its natural environment. Meadowview Heights appears to me to be an authentic, latter-day expression of the classical American style: simple, easily understood, and not without elegance. It is easy to criticize its monotony, its unimaginative siting, its deliberate avoidance of picturesque variety; but groups of houses similar to this one have always proliferated in the United States; Plymouth in the seventeenth century was such a one; the frontier outpost, the railroad town, the company town were others. We produce them by instinct.

So the change which Meadowview Heights exemplified seems to be little more than a reaffirmation of American Classicism. Except for one characteristic: none of the houses is of more than one story. The traditional hierarchy of floors, honored in even the simplest of traditional American dwellings—cellar, ground floor, attic—has been done away with.

Thus the housing development is also part of the spatial transformation; but in what manner? How does Meadowview Heights, brand new and efficiently planned, explain the struggle against spatial obsolescence so manifest in other parts of the town? The multistoried downtown "block" is abandoned; the multistoried residence is converted into a series of one-story flats; the multistoried barn with its silos is abandoned in favor of the one-story cement block structure; and the new houses in the development are of one story only. What explanation suffices for them all?

Clearly America is showing a preference for the horizontal over the vertical organization of space.

It would be more precise to say that Americans prefer to *work* on a horizontal plane, for the technological reasons for the shift are the most conspicuous. An efficiently planned office is now seen as a system of information flow, most flexible, most effective when horizontal. An industrial plant is likewise more efficient when its processes are horizontal, modern methods and equipment having largely eliminated gravity flow and difficulties of horizontal movement. This is no less true of the modern farm, where mobile machinery and electric power have greatly encouraged the horizontal layout and the abandonment of many vertical installations. Insofar as the contemporary dwelling is a highly mechanized structure, there too the horizontal flow, the horizontal organization of movement is preferred.

Everywhere the tendency to eliminate the vertical is evident. What at first sight seems an important exception—the enormous increase in the number of high-rise structures in our cities—is, I think, merely another and more complex form of horizontality. The modern multistoried office building differs from the earlier examples of the form in being essentially a stack of large, uninterrupted horizontal spaces: vastly improved construction methods have made this spaciousness possible. Exterior similarity between the old high rise and the new can be deceptive.

We have surely not reached the end of spatial transformation; and though it is in the city and in the industrial installation that horizontally produces its most sensational examples—strip mining being one of them—the small town contains its own share: the supermarket, the shopping center, the motel, the one-story consolidated high school, the one-story hospital, however commonplace they now may be, are still new and are still being built to replace the old vertical counterpart. The coming of the trench silo on the farm no doubt presages the development of the horizontal grain elevator; the landscape will be the poorer for the substitution.

I am not certain that the technological explanation for the change is the only one. An esthetic explanation could also be proposed. It is evident that Americans now perceive their environment in a new and as yet undefined manner. It is evident that increased mobility, and even more, an increased experience of uninterrupted speed—whether on the highway or the ski slope or on the surface of the water—bring with them a sharpened awareness of horizontal space and the eventual transformation of many landscapes devoted to recreation.

It is changes such as these—fragmentary and pragmatic—that we should look for when we explore the American landscape. They are widespread and consequently inconspicuous; we shall soon see them wherever we go and learn to accept them as commonplace. This means, I think, that the traditional uniformity, the Classical sameness of America will not be altered. Indeed it may be reinforced; horizontally will be incorporated into the national style, a universal American characteristic. The study and understanding of landscape metamorphosis can nowhere better be undertaken than in the contemporary United States, but it has to be undertaken in the proper frame of mind; and this is largely a matter of recognizing and accepting our national landscape for what it is: something very different from the European.

Country Towns for a
New Part of the Country

Courthouse and grid system, Plainview, Texas. (Photo: Lester Williams)

In the seventeenth century, when Englishmen began coming to the New World to live, they distinguished between a town and a city not on a basis of size or density or wealth, but on the role that each kind of settlement played. A city was thought of as the seat of authority. It was the place where the government had its headquarters, where the church was centered, the place where society was organized in a hierarchy of power and position. It was the symbol of the commonwealth, of dignity and permanence. That was one reason why Governor Winthrop hoped that the Puritan colony would become "as a city up on a hill."

Yet Boston was established as a town. A town was a collection of farms or dwellings, much the same as a parish. A New England town, in theory at least, meant a sizeable piece of prospective farmland of thirty-six square miles, and it often included not only many farms and homesteads but several small villages. In western Massachusetts there is a sign which says: "Town of Montague. Village Limits of Montague City."

In colonial Virginia, where there were never many villages and where people lived at some distance from one another, the word *city* was used to indicate any settlement of no matter what size that was a center of administration. At the very beginning the colonists decided there would be four or five such cities: Henrico City, Elizabeth City, Jamestown, and eventually Williamsburg, but they used the word in what to us seems a peculiar way. They talked about "the city in Jamestown," "the City at Enrico." There is something bewildering about how Americans, and especially Southerners, think of place names. In Virginia there is a small place called Elizabeth City County Courthouse—which is almost as hard to interpret as the street name in Baltimore: Charles Street Avenue Boulevard. The way we use the words no doubt signifies a change in how we define both *town* and *city*. Commonly we find businesses called Car Wash City, Surplus City, Buick City. What do we mean by that? A place were there is a concentration of some type of services or some type of goods.

Perhaps we are beginning to define the city itself as a place where there is an unusual concentration of goods and services. A contemporary definition of the town is hard to come by, and we almost always refer not to the town, but to the *small* town as a social and cultural entity, a definite type of community with special social and cultural and economic characteristics. Yet size has little to do with the definition, and indeed *small* town and *country* town are often interchangeable concepts. I myself would tentatively define such a town as one which has close ties with the surrounding countryside.

Early in its history Tidewater Virginia was divided into counties. These were small and sparsely populated, but each county had to have a courthouse. Where was the best place to put it? The solution was to place it as near as possible to the center of the county or at an important crossroads. Thus the early settlers, without realizing what they were doing, created one of the

73

most charming features of the colonial landscape: the formal brick courthouse, surrounded by lawn and trees, out in the empty countryside. Virginians even in those days were gregarious and social minded, yet they lived far
apart, and it was hard to pay calls on neighbors when there were rivers and
marshes to cross. The monthly sessions of the county court, the yearly elections, and the paying of taxes served as reasons for everyone coming together
at the courthouse. Men and women and children, tired of their lonely homes
and of hoeing tobacco, gathered from all around the county for a holiday and
to see friends. They came in wagons or on horseback or on foot—hunters,
backwoodsmen, small farmers, and rich plantation owners; paid their debts,
sold or bought anything from shovels to pieces of land, and when there was
an election under way, listened to the speeches and drank the free liquor
which the candidates provided.

The common people of colonial Virginia loved their courthouse just as
New Englanders loved their church. But what made the courthouse a valuable element in the landscape was not simply that it brought people together
to celebrate, it was a political institution. It was where people debated issues
and discussed county affairs. In that sense, the courthouse was the local
equivalent of a "city" in the Classical meaning of the word: "civitas": a
collection of citizens.

This courthouse place of assembly, as a kind of city, had its social hierarchy
too: those who could not vote and those who could; those who held office
and those who did not. It had its group of the rich and powerful, and its
majority of poor and ignorant people.

The Virginians were so fond of their courthouses that when they started to
move into what is now Kentucky and Tennessee, they took the courthouse
with them, and very soon the new landscape had its new counties and its log
cabin courthouses, and it was not long before the new settlers and the land
speculators among them began laying out towns to serve as centers. Farmers
were already raising commercial crops and needed markets; the sale of land
and the unending flow of newcomers to the region demanded the services of
lawyers and surveyors, and the offices of the land bureau. There was need for
teachers and clergymen. In many of the new planned towns, a courthouse
was therefore essential.

Early in the nineteenth century there developed the practice of laying out
new towns in the South meant to be county seats. Real estate operators and
speculators set aside a block of land in the center of the town, and often
donated it to the community as a site for a courthouse, and eventually a
typical southern courthouse town plan evolved.

A wonderfully complete study of courthouse towns was made several years
ago by E. T. Price, professor of geography at the University of Oregon.[1]
There are more than three thousand counties in the United States, each with

its county seat and its courthouse, and Professor Price visited them all. The courthouse squares are of several different kinds. In Pennsylvania and Ohio and West Virginia and Kentucky courthouses are frequently located at the intersection of two streets, and these are known as Philadelphia or Lancaster courthouse squares, after the two earliest eighteenth-century examples. The southern type square is merely one block in the center of a town composed of uniform rectangular blocks, for this was thought to be the logical place. The first county seat where the courthouse was deliberately located on a block by itself in or near the center of town was Shelbyville, Tennessee, in 1819.

In a few decades the Shelbyville plan had appeared as far north as Iowa and Missouri, as far east as South Carolina, and as far south as Texas, where in fact we find the most beautiful examples. Whoever has traveled through the upper South or the Gulf South will be familiar with courthouse towns. The courthouses dominate their surroundings with a tower or dome and an elaborate stone or brick facade. They are often extraordinary specimens of nineteenth-century public architecture, and although one time I regretted the destruction of any of them, I have since learned to accept it. Even court-houses dating from twenty or ten years ago have a remarkable monu-mentality, and in a generation or so will no doubt be studied by architectural historians.

In my travels I have seen many of these country towns with courthouses, and I think of them as having once played much the same social and political role as did the courthouses of colonial Virginia, though to be sure the setting is now urban. I would say the smaller the town, the more effective as a gathering place the courthouse has been. The square around it was usually occupied by small, locally owned retail stores; the movie theater, the small hotel, the barbershop, the cafe or restaurant where the town businessmen ate their lunch were all there and there was always a corner bank. Idle men, many of them old, sat on the courthouse steps or on benches in the shade of trees. I do not think of it as a space where there were many women. There were monuments on the lawn surrounding the building, and no matter how shab-by or how uninspired architectually it might have been the courthouse domi-nated its setting. I know of no other urban composition in the United States that is so picturesque, so dignified, and so sightly.

But to repeat what I said about the Virginia courthouse: the importance of the nineteenth-century courthouse was that it served as a political institution for making citizens. The courthouse was, of course, useful to the economy of the town. It brought farmers in from the surrounding countryside on legal or tax matters, it provided space for a weekly market, and concentrated the retail business with a conveniently compact area. But more than that, it was a place for discussion, for speeches, for celebration. Above all it was a place where the social variety of the town was on display: politicians, businessmen, and lawyers and social figures went in and out and were watched from a respectful distance. This was the hub, the focal point, not only of the town, but of the surrounding landscape.

What I am describing is a glimpse of the past. So it may not be inappropriate to quote from a description of a typical Alabama country town written some seventy-five years ago by Clifton Johnson, an itinerant photographer and the author of several charming books about his travels in rural America at the turn of the century.

> The town is widestreeted, and placid, with a broad public square at its heart, bounded by brick and wooden stores, law offices, etc. These structures are one and two stories high, and are pretty sure to have projecting from their fronts, across the sidewalk, an ample board roof to furnish shade; and between the supports of the roof, on the outside of the walk, is usually a plank seat. The walk is a good deal encumbered with displays of various goods, and here and there are huddles of empty whiskey barrels and other receptacles. The barrels and boxes, in common with the plank seats and sundry doorsteps and benches, are utilized very generally by loungers. The populace like to sit and consider, and they like to take their ease when talking with their friends. . . . A more aristocratic loitering place than provided by chance or intention as adjuncts of the stores, is a group of chairs at the rear door of the courthouse. Every pleasant day these chairs are brought out into the shadow of the building and the nearby trees, where they are occupied by some of the village worthies for the purpose of mild contemplation and discussion. . . . The business square on which the courthouse looks out from its enthroning trees with serene though antiquated dignity is usually very quiet. The town life is not very energetic. A good many of the stores get along without sign boards, and I frequently heard their proprietors whiling away their leisure in the recesses of their shops with a guitar, or cornet, or fiddle. . . . Saturday is, however, an exception. That is market day, and the public ways and hitching places are then crowded with mules and horses, many of them merely saddled, others attached to vehicles . . . ox teams are common, and once in a while a negro drives a single ox harnessed between his cart-shafts.[2]

I can remember many such country towns from the early days of my travels. I remember the handsome, spacious residential streets shaded by large trees and bordered by white houses with great porches. Somewhere near the center was often a small sectarian college, a composition of old-fashioned brick buildings, somewhat down at the heel, as if student life were a perpetual vacation and the college endowment little more than a dozen farms, raising corn or hay. Below the hill toward the depot was the black section of town in a tangle of vines, and there was a wide brown river where men fished all day long. I remember the good southern food at the restaurant on the square, the sound of hymn singing coming from every church Wednesday night; and above all, I remember with pleasure the general sense of completeness, as if the town had achieved its purpose of producing contented, well-behaved people and had decided not to grow or change.

Not to grow or change means in America to run the risk of decay and ultimate death: when did this paralysis set in? It was undoubtedly when the country town ceased to play its political role as "city." But that was more than a generation ago. Let me mention another kind of courthouse town or county seat, one that is probably less familiar to travelers in the East.

I mean the much newer, much less beautiful courthouse towns that have developed over the last decades in the High Plains country. There are numerous counties in Texas—to be exact, 254 of them. Many are small. One ranch stretches over parts of ten counties: the celebrated XIT Ranch—Ten in Texas. There are also many medium-size counties in western Kansas, eastern New Mexico, and throughout the High Plains and the Rockies all the way to the Canadian border. Few of them have a large population. Until recently they were chiefly engaged in ranching and wheat farming, with most of the inhabitants living near or at the county seat—a town with perhaps five or six thousand people. Over the past decade, however, many have come to life and a degree of prosperity, thanks, very often, to the discovery and exploitation of a valuable natural resource—oil or gas or uranium or coal—or to a new irrigation project, or an Army post.

These small towns, unlike those in the East, have expanded in a relatively orderly manner and have in some cases become communities of promise. In many ways they resemble the traditional southern county seat, but interestingly, they have developed a morphology and even a way of life of their own; for none of them plays the traditional role of producing citizens, or even tries to.

None of them departs from the established American grid layout—except where there are small, prosperous, semiurban residential developments. The grid is more conspicuous here because the terrain is level and there are few tall trees. The streets are broader, and only two or three of them bear historical names. East and west they are numbered, north and south they are given letters of the alphabet—or the system is reversed. There are dozens of identical rectangular blocks bordered by neat, rectangular, one-story houses, each with its bright green lawn and with a pickup truck parked in front. There are rows of small Chinese elms or Russian olives waving in the incessant wind. In time they will grow into trees of some size, but now they scarcely cast a shadow. It is only in the oldest part of town, down by the depot and beyond the railroad tracks that we glimpse what the place was like a half century ago, when it was little more than a village where men worked for the railroad. Here there are dilapidated frame houses with large trees and yards full of tricycles and old cars. Almost everywhere you look you see the immense surrounding landscape. Sometimes there are oil pumps, slowly nodding. There is little color in the view, but when a cloud briefly hides the sun there are brilliant contrasts of light and shadow.

For three or four blocks Main Street is lined with retail business establish-

ments, and the courthouse square (a block in the center of town following
the old southern custom) is likewise lined with small, modest, one-story
buildings: post office, newspaper, one of the several banks, beautician, men's
wear, and so on. These are not handsome specimens of architecture, but they
are practical. As we know, the small American town, even the small American
city, can no longer support three- or four-story buildings in the business
section. No small business, no office, no agency ever wants to be up a flight
of stairs. One of the depressing sights in the traditional courthouse square is
the number of vacant or boarded up windows in the second and third stories
of the old brick buildings. The new towns in the High Plains have managed
to avoid this blight, and architects wishing to revitalize the small downtown
area could, I think, be more profitably employed in designing—or redesign-
ing—these one-story offices and stores to give them something like style,
than in trying to preserve or rehabilitate the few two- or three-story buildings
which survive.

As for the courthouse itself, it has dignity because of its isolation and bulk,
and it is in fact the only structure in town with architectural pretensions.
Even so, it is modern enough in spirit to betray the contemporary attitude
toward public buildings: they are no longer designed as palaces or monuments. They are treated as office buildings and they have no dome or tower;
no columns. The open space surrounding them is planted to grass. There is
seldom a statue or a monument or even an historic marker. Several decades
ago there was a movement, doubtless well intentioned, to give a replica of the
Statue of Liberty, five feet high, to every town which had done its share in
World War I. The Boy Scouts of America were responsible for this gener-
osity, but in the course of years the statues have deteriorated, sometimes
losing their head, and I imagine they will soon disappear altogether. Probably
because it offers little shade and is somewhat isolated from pedestrian traffic,
the square does not seem a place for loitering. The new courthouse has little
symbolic value. What stands out on the skyline of the town are the grain
elevators, the screen of the drive-in movie, and the water tower. After dark
there are few bright lights except for the vapor lights along Main Street and
the red-and-green lights of the string of motels.

Is there any element of the old or picturesque? I think not. There are no
recognizable architectural antiquities, nothing worth preserving and restoring. The oldest residence of any character dates from perhaps 1910, and it is
either well-preserved in the form of a funeral home or it is in a state of
imminent collapse. In many of these remote, isolated towns the state highway
runs down Main Street, creating the illusion of traffic and encouraging a
certain amount of drive-in business, but usually these are towns you drive
through at 45 MPH. You scarcely notice them, they interrupt so briefly the
experience of empty sunlit space.

Yet they have features which seem effective in producing on a modest scale an illusion of community life, and these I think could be encouraged. If the courthouse square is not the most important gathering place, there are several substitutes. Because of the overgenerous scale of their layout, the towns have many vacant spaces serving as playgrounds and potential parks. There is usually a poorly maintained rodeo ground, and the school provides a football field and a baseball diamond and an informal picnic area. Shopping centers are, to be sure, part of every American town, but in these western communities, where they are rarely landscaped, the great expanse of parking areas, the canopies over the fronts of the stores are places of sociability and even the scene of such popular events as the arrival of Santa Claus in a helicopter, the oratory of political candidates, the display of new model cars. In the store windows you find announcements of bake sales, garage sales, revivals, ballet lessons.

Finally, there is one gathering space that is without parallel in towns in the older parts of the country: the strip development along the highway at both ends of Main Street. The strip often is not only an ugly and offensive part of town, but inefficient as well, and it is its inefficiency and lack of order that disturb its critics and the general public. Yet the strip serves an important function in the American community. It is hardly necessary to point to the importance of the automobile in our life, and in rural or semirural areas our dependence on the automobile is magnified; we could not survive without it. There has to be an area where we can easily go to have the truck or automobile serviced, where the truck or automobile can be bought or sold, and where the several aspects of automobile usage are taken care of. Before we condemn the anarchy of the strip we should ask ourselves if we would prefer to have it scattered in fragments throughout our towns and cities? Repair shops, sales lots, garages can be noisy, dirty, crowded places with much coming and going, and they demand a great deal of space. Is it not better to have these auto-related establishments located on both sides of a wide thoroughfare where there is already heavy traffic?

The strip, moreover, is more than an area devoted to the sale and servicing of trucks and automobiles. In many parts of America where large-scale technology is invading the countryside it is fast becoming the place where specialized equipment is serviced and sold and where, in consequence, we are likely to find specialized skills. This is where we see the immense displays of brightly colored, mechanized farm equipment. In regions of mining and drilling and irrigation and large-scale construction, this is where we find engineering firms and services. The out-of-town worker or foreman comes here to find talent and help in maintaining or repairing his equipment. It is perhaps too much to say that the strip in the rural center is the focus of expertise, but it is where we find certain skills and certain products which the town itself does not need but which the countryside must have. What we see, more and more, are gatherings of field workers and mechanics and construction foremen along the strip. The motels and restaurants are often crowded with men who have come to town in search of help, and motels are even serving as small conference centers where new ideas, new problems, new solutions in the world of technology are exchanged. I know of no more vital area in the town; and a well-equipped, well-planned, versatile strip is what these new towns depend on to attract outsiders and to maintain contact with the rural economy. And above all, this kind of strip helps provide jobs for the young.

The strip is not only the locus of the automobile economy, not only the technological center, it is also the place where young people go for pleasure. It was the South, I think, that first discovered the attractions of the strip; it was here that the younger generation first learned to spend its leisure cruising from one drive-in to another. This is a noisy and often extravagant way of passing the evening, but by and large it is as good a form of recreation as we can offer to small-town youth. Is it not an improvement over the old-fashioned horse culture of the past? From what we learn of that culture it was vicious and disreputable: concentrated in back alleys and in livery stables, dirty, inefficient, and frequented by the sorriest element in the population; the object of widespread and probably justified disapproval. This cannot be said of the strip. Eating junk food and showing off may not be a profitable pastime, but it is relatively harmless, it has nothing surreptitious or furtive about it. Those who recommend that the strip as a place of entertainment and of transient accommodations should be separated from the strip as place of work and business have a point. But we need to analyze the strip, its hazards and opportunities, before we undertake to control it or abolish it.

If these small new towns without cultural pretensions and (it should be added) without any clear vision of their future possess any qualities worth emulating, we should admire their broad streets, their large lots, their low density; their spacious, relaxed layout. I think their strip development suggests a better way to organize the industrial aspects of the urban morphology—hitherto of necessity concentrated near the railroad tracks. A third advantage of these towns in the High Plains is their housing. The working man, transient or permanent, lives better here than he does in the older communities. This has not come about as the result of any enlightened policy or program. It comes in large part from the fact that land was once cheap, and that in colder or brisker climates houses are stoutly built and provided with utilities. It comes from the fact that unlike the older towns of the South and East these newer towns built few speculative dwellings for unskilled labor. I am thinking of the remarkable collection of shotgun houses in Greenwood, Mississippi, block after block of one-story frame houses, one room wide and three rooms long, put up, as I understand it, to accommodate the unskilled labor employed in the cotton industry, and now entirely occupied by blacks. When they were built they seemed adequate—at least to the builders. In the

West, however, new houses are either of the prefabricated, mail-order variety or made of cement block, for lack of inexpensive lumber. The current solution to the problem of rapid population growth is the mobile home—or what is often called manufactured housing. This is not a form of dwelling likely to be popular with Easterners, but the appeal of the trailer community is not so much visual as it is the better, more spacious quality of domestic life and the temporary nature of the groups. Instead of creating an ever-deteriorating slum, the neighborhood composed of mobile homes usually disappears or disintegrates.

I have been discussing the nature of small urban places in the South and East largely with the idea of our keeping them alive. Let us hope that this can and will be done. But we should also consider which traditional traits—social as well as environmental—are best suited to transplanting and perpetuating in the New West. I can think of several traditional characteristics that should be incorporated in any new town: a kind of self-sufficiency and independence of metropolitan ways, a solidarity and sense of kinship among people, an intimate and affectionate relationship with the immediate rural surroundings and with those who live there, and lastly a respect for local history and its monuments, and an awareness of corporate dignity.

On the other hand, there are old-fashioned civic traits which are clearly not to be carried over into the future: entrenched class and racial distinctions, a dependence on an old-fashioned, inefficient agriculture, a disdain for experimentation, and a nostalgic attitude toward a long-vanished past.

In physical terms, all our new towns in the West will be larger and more populous. A generation ago it was generally thought that a country town could survive if it had such facilities as a high school, a hospital, a supermarket, a radio station, and a variety of professions and trades; and that such a town could support these facilities with a population of no more than 10,000. I imagine that that figure should now be at least doubled. One reason is that the basic relationship between town and countryside is changing. The rural environment is playing a very different and much more demanding role. It is both the place where much of the active population goes to work—in construction or processing or mining or in highly mechanized forms of agriculture—and the places where people go for recreation: fishing, boating, hunting, rock hunting, camping, and exploring. Yet even with this radical change, the traditional definition holds: a small country town can still be a community where people are brought together by living near one another, where they freely work together and celebrate together. It can still be a community where existence can be made more complete by close and frequent contact with the rural setting.

Vernacular

Street on edge of town, Cushing, Oklahoma. (Photo: Harold Corsini)

The increasing interest among architects in what we call vernacular architecture and the growing public awareness of a rich vernacular heritage suggest that it is time we examine the nature of the vernacular and its historical development.

As generally used, the word suggests something countrified, homemade, traditional. As used in connection with architecture, it indicates the traditional rural or small-town dwelling, the dwelling of the farmer or craftsman or wage earner. Current definitions of the word usually suggest that the vernacular dwelling is designed by a craftsman, not an architect, that it is built with local techniques, local materials, and with the local environment in mind: its climate, its traditions, its economy—predominantly agricultural. Such a dwelling does not pretend to stylistic sophistication. It is loyal to local forms and rarely accepts innovations from outside the region. It is not subject to fashion and is little influenced by history in its wider sense. That is why the word *timeless* is much used in descriptions of vernacular building.

This definition is largely the product of architects and architectural historians, hence the emphasis on form and building techniques and the relative neglect of function or of the relationship to work and community. In fact architectural scholars may be said to have discovered the vernacular and to have done much of the early research into its characteristics. The current definition has been very serviceable. Nevertheless it should be noted that it derives for the most part from the mid-nineteenth-century exploration of rural life by antiquarians and those dissatisfied with urban, industrialized life. Of late years the study of vernacular building has been greatly influenced by speculations on the psychology and mythology of traditional man-made spaces. It owes much to the interpretations of Jung and Eliade and Bachelard and even Heidegger, none of whom was much concerned with the economic or political aspects of the dwelling.

But other disciplines also have been involved in studying the vernacular. Much work has been done by geographers, social historians, and archeologists, and they have contributed to a broader, more prosaic definition of vernacular architecture that we cannot afford to ignore. To put it briefly, what they have done is to reveal that vernacular building, especially in Europe, has had a history of its own, distinct from that of formal architecture, and that far from being "timeless" and determined by ancient archetypes, it has undergone a long and complicated evolution.

What chiefly concerns us as Americans are the more recent chapters in that European chronicle of vernacular buildings—roughly from the sixteenth century onward. (The usual cutoff date is the mid-nineteenth century.) A period once thought of as the heyday of the so-called timeless forms of vernacular architecture—the sixteenth and seventeenth and early eighteenth centuries—has now been revealed as a period of far-reaching changes, not only in the design and construction of the dwelling, but in its economic and social functions and even in its legal definition. This fateful period corresponds of course to the period when the first colonists from Atlantic Europe arrived in North America. They brought with them, in other words, a revolution in vernacular architecture, and it was here in the New World that that revolution has been carried through to the present.

This is not the place to discuss the origins of that revolution. We need only recall the Enclosure Movement in England, the growing scarcity of wood, the development of planned communities throughout Europe, the coming of manufacturing, and above all what Philippe Ariès calls "the discovery of the child," to realize that a new type of dwelling with new uses *had* to evolve. It was, even in Europe, a type which did not conform to that popular academic definition which we still use. It was not simply rural and agricultural, it was identified with mining and shipping communities, with cities and the architect- or engineer-planned villages having a military or political function. Finally it used materials and techniques imported from elsewhere. And yet because it was an architecture meant for farmers or craftsmen or wage earners it still qualified—and is still thought of—as vernacular.

Many of these novelties were brought to America by the settlers and the colonial authorities. What gave this imported vernacular its uniquely American quality was the abundance of wood for construction, the abundance of land, the rapid increase in the young population, and the scarcity of skilled labor. Out of this combination of Old World and New World factors came a vernacular style characterized by short-lived or temporary dwellings focused on the family and distinct from the place of work, dwellings largely independent of the traditional community constraints and institutions, dwellings using new construction techniques, and with a new relationship to the environment.

Can we write a history of the American vernacular dwelling in terms of these and similar traits? I think we can. The temporary or movable dwelling has been a feature of the American landscape ever since colonial times. The dwelling as an environment for the child-centered family, urban as well as rural, has inspired the replanning of the dwelling, the increase in the number of rooms, and the introduction of utilities and conveniences long before they were introduced in Europe. The American vernacular home, designed as a microenvironment, is dependent on the community not as a political entity but as a source of services, and we have accordingly developed settlement forms of a nonpolitical sort: the suburb, the company town, the trailer court, the resort area, and the condominium.

The structural innovations which our vernacular architecture has introduced are well covered in every architectural history: the log cabin, the balloon frame, the box house, the ready-cut, or prefabricated, house, and the mobile home. But a chapter yet to be written by historians would deal with the vast amount of modification and improvement, interior as well as exterior, that almost every American householder undertakes. Thanks to our tradition of building with wood, and thanks also to the recent introduction of power tools, we are becoming a nation of amateur carpenters and electricians, not always knowing when to leave well enough alone.

I hope I am aware of some of the shortcomings of contemporary American vernacular architecture. Compared to traditional, pretechnological dwellings ours are spiritually and culturally impoverished. Our almost uncontrollable love of making "environments"—never stronger than now—compels us to create in our houses as well as in our cities environments that are good for nothing but health and recreation, environments almost entirely without content. And I know how fatally easy it is for us to produce short-lived communities composed of flimsy and undistinguished architecture. It is certainly part of any study of American vernacular to point out these and other mistakes and to remind us how they were avoided in the past. At the same time we would do well, at least in the beginning, to avoid passing easy, subjective judgments. A prosaic, conscientious, and reasonably sympathetic study of our wonderful profusion of vernacular architecture—a profusion that shows no signs of abating—would lead to a better understanding of many aspects of everyday America and how they came into being.

The origin of a word often throws a new light on the way we use it. Take the word *dwelling*. If we are using it as a noun—if we are speaking of the dwelling as a house—we should really say, "dwelling place." The verb *to dwell* has a distinct meaning. At one time it meant to hesitate, to linger, to delay, as when we say, "He is dwelling too long on this insignificant matter." *To dwell,* like the verb *to abide* (from which we derive *abode*), simply means to pause, to stay put for a length of time; it implies that we will eventually move on. So the dwelling place should perhaps be seen as temporary. Our being in it is contingent on many external factors.

How long do we have to stay in a place for it to become a dwelling? That may seem an unimportant question, yet I think we should try to answer it. I would say we stay long enough for our presence to become customary. A place becomes a dwelling when it is part of our customary behavior. To stay there overnight or even two or three nights will not do. But when we stay there because we have a steady job or are a student then it becomes an element in a customary or habitual way of life.

This way of defining the word is born out by the usage of the verb *to dwell* in other languages. In English (it is hard to see why) we say "live" in a place. Both French and German retain the equivalent of *to dwell* and find it very serviceable. In French you do not say, "Où vivez vous?" you say "Où habitez vous?" Just as in German you do not say, "Wo leben Sie?" but "Wo wohnen Sie?" Both expressions imply an habitual action, and indeed both of them are closely related to the words for custom or habit: *habitude* and *Gewohnheit*.

This usage suggests a certain detachment from the dwelling. Habits and customs are of course important and often very pleasant, but we do not think of them as really basic elements of our existence. They are adapted, they are acquired, but they are also discarded when we tire of them. And this is true also of the contemporary dwelling. No matter how comfortable or convenient it may be, we know that the time may well come when we find it wise to change: this is perhaps the best moment to sell. Perhaps a new job demands that we move or the neighborhood threatens to deteriorate or the children have grown up and left home. So we look for another dwelling; and since other people feel the same, another suitable dwelling is not usually hard to find.

What I am suggesting is that the home and the dwelling are two separate things, though they usually coincide. This truth is obvious to all modern Americans, but I believe that there was a time when people did not make this distinction.

This brings me to a second word. *Chattel,* an article of personal, movable property, is related to *cattle* and to *capital,* but the relationship with *cattle* is the older of the two. At a remote time in Roman history all land and all power belonged to the family or clan or tribe. The only thing corresponding to individual private property was the few head of cattle (or sheep) which the man of the household grazed on common land. What made this property desirable was that it could be disposed of without consulting the larger group. The cattle could be accumulated and bought and sold and given to any son or daughter the man chose. Cattle were negotiable and could be translated into cash, and one reason they were negotiable was that they were mobile, they could be moved. So they represented two very important freedoms: freedom from the authority of the community and freedom from territorial or environmental constraints.

In the course of centuries many more things were defined as chattels, and in the Middle Ages the dwelling was likewise defined as chattel under certain conditions. This meant that it could be disposed of independent of the land to which it was often closely tied. If according to established laws of inheritance a man was legally obliged to leave his land to his eldest son he could, if he wanted to, leave his dwelling to his widow or to his daughter or to the church. As the word *movable* implied, he could also move it to another site. But this did not hold true of all dwellings: usually only the more modest kind, those built of wood, could be separated from the operation of the farm. The farm or the estate itself could not be alienated—that is to say, disposed of—for it was to descend to his children.

This notion that the dwelling was independent of the land and was legally (and even literally) mobile naturally produced a distinctive kind of dwelling, particularly in towns and cities: houses which were built to be rented or used for a variety of profitable purposes. They tended to be simple in construction and uniform. We can think of those early rental units as the medieval equivalent of the contemporary trailer—not only in their mobility but in their standardization and construction and in their appeal to working-class families with a job somewhere nearby.

But there were from the earliest times two types of houses. The dwelling was, of course, much more numerous, but the other kind is the kind which architectural historians usually know more about. To greatly oversimplify, we can say that this second kind was in many ways the complete opposite of the first. It was identified with a family over generations—so much so that another term for a dynasty is *house*—like the house of Windsor or the house of Rothschild. It was as large and as permanent as possible because it was a symbol of power and status in the community. It was not uncommon for town and city authorities to prescribe the size and design of the houses of the rich and powerful and to insist on a certain grandeur in appearance. Furthermore, there were features to these houses which clearly indicated the rank of the occupying family: the presence of a tower or dungeon meant that the occupant was a judge of a certain type of court of justice. I need not say much more about these houses except to repeat that they were built of stone. Both words—*manor* and *mansion*—derive from a root meaning lasting, enduring, and in Wales the word for such a house—whether a manor or a prosperous homestead—included the word *stone*. Architectural history naturally has more to say about these houses than about the peasant or worker dwelling. For one thing the so-called mansion has usually been protected by the family, and its history is a matter of record. For another, the various symbolic features—tower, dungeon, moat, courtyard, ceremonial entrance—eventually become elements in an architectural style. But the most striking difference is this: whereas the dwelling by its very poverty has few ways of preserving and providing for the long-range future, the mansion is deeply involved in both concerns. It is at once a monument to the history of the family and its power and wealth and a legacy for future generations to honor and preserve.

Much of the story of domestic architecture in the Western world, and especially in America, can be written in terms of the contrast between these two kinds of houses. Clearly there is a class distinction between the point of view of the family of wealth and position and that of the family of job seekers and job holders perpetually on the move. There is also an obvious distinction, transcending class, between two ways of honoring the past and the future, of thinking of history. But the distinction which I find most interesting in America is a much simpler one: the distinction between the house built to last, built as a permanent part of the environment, and the house with a life expectancy of a generation or less, the house which serves a limited purpose in the lives of its occupants.

In other words, what I think worth exploring is the fluctuating fortunes of stone and wood as building materials; specifically the low standing of wood in medieval Europe, its almost total rejection during the Renaissance, and its triumphant reemergence in America. We should explore the development of the dwelling and how we made it the standard house, part of the standard way of life, of the United States.

Our American housing tradition derives from seventeenth- and eighteenth-century England, but ultimately from what is sometimes called Atlantic Europe—that forested region of Europe north of the Alps and north of the Loire. Atlantic Europe thus includes Scandinavia, Germany, England, the Lowlands, and northern France. A thousand years ago, despite the influence of the Roman Empire, this was still a rural landscape, largely covered by forests and moor. It was therefore a region of wooden houses and a region where there was a flourishing culture of wood. This culture persists in many different forms in contemporary America, and in one way or another most Americans take part in it.

We enjoy being part-time carpenter and repairman, patching up a structure we secretly know will eventually collapse or go up in flames. Perhaps we really enjoy wood's temporary quality; that is what makes it seem alive and responsive.

I suspect this has always been the case; we seem always to have built our wooden dwellings rapidly and with the idea that we can eventually change and improve—or abandon them. Archeologists tell us that though medieval carpentry techniques were highly developed in the building of boats and bridges and churches, the construction of the average peasant dwelling was slipshod and entirely without art. Few dwellings were expected to last more than a dozen years, and it was not unheard of for men to set fire to their own houses by way of holiday celebration. They could easily be replaced. All that was worth salvaging were the four cornerposts, beams, and rafters. The mud and brush walls, the thatch roof, and the few items of furniture were quickly reproduced. Americans lament that their houses are not allowed to grow old, and in fact the age of the average American is greater than that of the house he lives in. But even so our houses last much longer than did those of our medieval ancestors.

Impermanence was thus the chief characteristic of those early wooden constructions. A second characteristic was mobility. It was simple to disassemble a dwelling which was little more than a crude frame of a half dozen posts and beams and which had no foundation, no floor, and no ceiling. Many medieval accounts tell of dwellings being moved to where the next job was or onto a patch of vacant land. Whole villages moved when the soil was exhausted or when they were threatened by enemy attack. The image of the peasant family rooted for generations in the same spot is being modified by modern historians. As we will see, it is better suited to the peasant of the Renaissance or even of the nineteenth century than to the peasant of the Middle Ages.

The peasant of Atlantic Europe appears to have been very loyal to the tradition of the wooden dwelling, even in regions where wood was scarce and stone or clay was plentiful, and something of that loyalty was carried over to America in the seventeenth century. Jefferson complained that ignorant Virginians objected to brick houses for reasons of health, and as late as 1795 the Salem diarist William Bentley noted that the house of a certain Mr. Lee "was demolished from the prejudice against brick houses."

But the preference for wood was not shared by the more prosperous classes. The medieval clergy and the medieval aristocracy were outspoken in their admiration of stone. The theological doctrines which endorsed stone and masonry were extremely learned, and in their time no doubt very convincing.

The schism in architectural design lasted throughout the Middle Ages, with neither point of view getting the upper hand. But beginning in the sixteenth century, masonry somewhat abruptly became much more general. The two most obvious reasons for the shift were the renewed interest in classical architecture inspired by travel to Italy and then a serious shortage of wood throughout Atlantic Europe. Many forests had been destroyed by a growing population, the increase in the size of cities demanded more and more timber, and so did the building of fleets of naval and commercial ships. Finally, there was a great demand for wood as fuel in manufacturing.

The response to these developments was a great change in building methods. There came a wave of conservation legislation: a limitation on the amount of wood peasants could use in construction, the use of different kinds of wood, and most important of all a movement to replace wooden structures by structures of stone or brick. Though it started with the building of handsome houses in the city, it soon extended to include village dwellings and even whole villages and towns. This housing revolution of the sixteenth and seventeenth centuries—which the English call the Great Rebuilding and the French call the Victory of Stone over Wood—had a drastic influence on the attitudes toward the dwelling. Simone Roux, in her recent historical survey of housing, says,

> It was the triumph of the heavy stone house, the Mediterranean solution imposed on the rest of Europe. . . . Here we were, reconstructing in stone that which we had originally built of wood and mud. A house weighing from four hundred to five hundred tons, meant to last for centuries without expensive upkeep, was hereafter to serve as a symbol of permanence, of solidity, of reassuring protection. It stood for the complete shelter, the perfect hearth or home, the guardian of generations of accumulated memories. The [masonry] house tied the family to the land; the heavy construction called for a large outlay of money, it represented a large investment in permanent prestige. The stone house, ideally adapted to the needs of a static society, became the center of innumerable small investments.[1]

No one can doubt that this reform in housing was by and large a benefit. The architectural revolution of the sixteenth and seventeenth centuries not only produced handsome cities and towns and palaces and mansions, it also replaced dark and unsanitary cottages with stone dwellings which were larger, better designed, and more sightly. Still, we must not lose sight of the virtues which were thereby outlawed. For all their squalor medieval peasant dwellings had a remarkable flexibility and mobility—not only in that they could be taken down and reassembled elsewhere, but also in that they could easily change function and change tenants. If their life span was brief it allowed for frequent replacement. When the old dwelling collapsed, the new one was apt to be better and was certain to be cleaner. And finally, the temporary nature of the dwelling, its negligible material value, meant that it could be lightheartedly abandoned when the crops failed, when war threatened, or when the local lord proved too demanding. Its flimsiness protected the family from dangers of staying put. If people could not fight misfortune, they could at least escape it by leaving house and environment behind.

The more we learn about that victory of stone over wood, the more one question seems to demand an answer: was colonial America likewise engulfed in the Mediterranean architectural tide? There was of course no great rebuilding in North America, for there was no building, no architectural tradition to begin with. But it is certainly true, as most histories of American architecture insist on telling us, that once the first harsh pioneer days were over, the well-to-do and ambitious colonists from Virginia to Maine started to build substantial urban and suburban houses in the fashionable style of the period. Tidewater Virginia came nearest to being overwhelmed by the new design philosophy. The eighteenth-century planters delighted in massive brick construction, and in fact the authorities in London in the middle of the seventeenth century ordained that every Virginia planter who owned a hundred acres had to build a brick house—with brick foundations—of specified dimensions. If he owned more than one hundred acres, his house had to be proportionately larger. What makes the history of the Tidewater area especially interesting is that it became the favorite target of the design innovators—much more than New England did. The strange constitution which John Locke drew up for South Carolina in the last years of the seventeenth century called for a baroque organization of space, and the design of Williamsburg was a model of Mediterranean order and would-be permanence.

But these attempts to produce a Renaissance landscape in colonial America came to nothing. In Virginia as in New England, the vast majority of dwellings were of wood, built by amateurs, and few of them were destined to last for many years. Of all the architectural historians, Alan Gowans is the one who has most eloquently described the medieval—or late medieval—quality of early American architecture.[2] I think most of us now agree with his verdict. The social and economic conditions in the colonies were totally different from those in Europe. Abundant land meant that every settler looked forward to a substantial allotment of ground and that dissatisfied settlers could move to new and more promising places after a few years. The immense forests provided wood for building; the absence of stone suitable for masonry (notably in Tidewater Virginia), the cost of making or importing brick, and above all the scarcity of skilled carpenters and joiners combined to foster the production of wooden houses that were often hastily put together, lacking in solid foundations, storage space, and weathered lumber. The result was a stock of small, cheaply built, short-lived wooden houses easily taken down or moved, easily modified, and designed to meet the pressing need for shelter in a pioneer landscape. But the real novelty of these dwellings was not that they were cheaply built and quickly moved or disassembled—those after all were the characteristics of the medieval cottage. The real novelty was that these dwellings were built, occupied, and eventually disposed of as *commodities,* merchandise designed and produced to satisfy a definite market.

What kind of market was that? In the seventeenth and eighteenth centuries it was a market composed of young, blue-collar families needing a place to live in a new environment. In those days this was assumed to be a farm, though in America it was a different kind of farm: not necessarily a permanent home, but rather merely a place of land which a family could exploit profitably for a number of years before moving on to where prospects seemed brighter: better soil, better returns, better neighbors.

For example, in his *Economic History of Virginia in the Seventeenth Century*, P. A. Bruce discusses the kind of house the first settlers built: a small, crude shelter with walls of vertical boards or slabs nailed to a horizontal board, and a pitched roof on top of the completed rectangle. The houses usually had two rooms, as well as a number of outhouses and barns and sheds. The farmer or planter at once started to raise tobacco. After two or three years he had exhausted the soil and there was nothing to do but move. Bruce comments:

> The inclination to abandon old plantations and to take up new ones . . . encouraged a more active destruction of the woods but at the same time it fostered a spirit of indifference as to the manner in which they used it. The [settlers] neglected the fencing of their grounds, they failed to establish pastures for their cattle, or to lay off orchards and gardens, and even to plant corn. So frail were many of the dwelling houses in consequence of the purpose of its occupants to desert their estates as soon as exhausted . . . that special instructions were sent to the Governor to discourage by every means in his power the erection of such temporary habitations.[3]

What we glimpse in this passage is the typical ramshackle frame house in the midst of abandoned fields that we find throughout contemporary America; and when we know America well, we find nothing really sad in the spectacle. The deserted house, nine times out of ten, is a chrysalis from which its inhabitants have happily escaped to some brighter or more alluring prospect. Only in the Old World, with its dream of permanence, does the deserted house or the deserted field invariably speak of human tragedy.

Several of the essential traits of the American dwelling appear in Bruce's description of early Virginia: the frailty, not to say the flimsiness, of its construction; the temporary quality, the indifference to the immediate environment, the loneliness—and of course the lavish, almost exclusive use of wood. I would add two further characteristics: the absence of storage space in the dwelling itself and the absence of a solid foundation. Finally there is a trait which we all take for granted but which few foreign observers can begin to understand: the remoteness of many farms and dwellings from any community.

Let us repeat the familiar story of the structural evolution of the classic American dwelling: not the architect-designed house or mansion (or whatever), but the type of shelter that most Americans live in. The first step was that makeshift slab house without foundation of the colonial South. The second step, dating from the early eighteenth century in Pennsylvania and, like the slab house, identified with the pioneer, frontier community, was the log cabin. It flourished in western Virginia and throughout the frontier South. Jefferson, whose architectural philosophy was definitely aristocratic and promasonry, described both types in his *Notes on the State of Virginia.* "The greatest proportion of the private buildings of Virginia are of scantling and boards, plastered with lime. It is impossible to devise things more ugly, uncomfortable, and happily more perishable." He adds: "The poorest people build huts of logs, laid horizontally in pens, stopping the interstices with mud. These are warmer in winter and cooler in summer than the more expensive construction of scantling and plank."[4]

Both types seem to have been generally temporary, to be succeeded in a matter of years by a more substantial house, and in both cases the plan was simplicity itself, with no provision for storage within the building, no foundation, no use of traditional carpentry skills, and no concern for appearances. Eventually the log cabin or slab house became a barn or was allowed to fall down. The third step was of course the balloon frame—another frontier invention. It represented a radical change in construction techniques, and yet at the same time it was a logical development: like its predecessors it was quick and simple to build, it was indifferent to local or folk architectural traditions, and it was seen as temporary; not that it would collapse, but that it would soon be sold and passed on to newcomers. Solon Robinson and other writers on western pioneering thus advised families to build their balloon frame houses as impersonally as possible so that they would be acceptable to any prospective purchaser. In the course of a few decades the balloon frame achieved architectural respectability, but even as late as 1870 a writer telling of his journey through Arkansas and Texas noted that there was scarcely any real architecture in that region since most of the buildings were balloon frame.

The acceptance of the balloon frame by serious architects can perhaps be explained by the development of two even simpler types of dwellings: the ready-cut or mail-order house, which flourished from the 1860s until the present and which has been studied by many architectural historians in recent years, and the simultaneous development of an even simpler type of dwelling—the box house.

Superficially—that is to say, from the outside—the box house resembles the board-and-batten house. But whereas the board-and-batten house usually has an insulating wall of brick under the exterior and a plastered interior wall, the true box house has no frame, no interior insulation, and of course no foundation. I have the feeling that it first developed in the Chesapeake Bay region. Long before the Civil War it had spread along the Gulf of Mexico and even as far as California. Horace Bushnell, a native of Hartford, Connecticut, was astonished to see box houses being built in San Francisco in the 1850s. Charles Dwyer, who wrote a book about low-cost housing in 1855, noted that workers on railroads and canals lived in settlements of box houses.

This is how the box house is described by Dianne Tebbetts in *Pioneer America:*

> Box construction is similar to plank construction that developed in medieval England. . . . In box construction . . . wide boards are nailed vertically [to sills laid on the ground] and a 2×4 is nailed horizontally along the top of these vertical boards. Additional vertical boards are attached to form a single thickness wall with *no framing at all.* Ceiling joists tie it together, and doors and windows sit in holes cut in the walls for them. . . . Inside the walls are usually heavily papered to keep out winter winds. What this manner of construction lacks in durability it makes up in economy, for it is the least expensive way to enclose a given volume. Box construction is fairly common throughout the Ozarks. . . . It is preferred as evidence of some prosperity over the sturdier log house. Accordingly the "hillman" who has money to spend prefers a box house of sawed native lumber with a cheap tarpaper roof.[5]

The New Mexico mining community of Madrid has a great many specimens of box houses. They were brought there in the 1920s from Tucumcari, two hundred miles away, where they had provided housing for workers on the Rock Island Railroad. I have yet to see a box house which is solid in appearance. The absence of any kind of frame saves money, but it allows the building to sag and bulge and reduces its overall strength. That is why the average box house is only one room wide and one story high. Inevitably it is associated with the poorest and most transient element in the population. Even today in much of the South it is usually called a rent house or a tenant house, and occasionally it is called a former slave cabin—even though few now standing are old enough to have accommodated slaves. I have a strong suspicion that many of the so-called frame buildings we see in pictures of the nineteenth-century boom mining towns were actually box houses. There was a time when the box house was one of the commonest types in the United States—far more common, I imagine, than the balloon frame. In the post–Civil War South the box house proliferated in lumber company towns, plantations, and railroad camps. The lumber towns, as might be imagined, produced them in great numbers, for the towns moved from place to place wherever the forest was exhausted, and they needed a mobile dwelling type.

An article on these towns and their architecture appeared in the *Geographical Review* for September 1957.[6] The writer identified at least three distinct types: the so-called bungalow (with a wide, encircling porch), the shotgun, and the log-pen house. The author suggested that the box house was popular in lumber towns because it was cheap and easy to build, suited to any size family, and easy to move by rail. The shotgun house, because of its narrowness (one room wide and two or more rooms deep), was well suited to small city lots and became very popular when moved to industrial cities.

The last chapter in the history of the box house tells of its use in remote company towns during the World War I, and then of its use for migrant farm workers in the South, the Southwest, and California. We know far less about its spread and its development than we should, because it is very much part of the new American landscape.

The growth of large-scale truck gardening in the Sunbelt states fostered the growth of a very mobile work force. In the years before World War I the average farm worker was a single man, variously called a tramp, a blanket-man, or a bindlestiff. He slept wherever he could. But in the 1920s sec-ondhand cars became relatively cheap, and instead of traveling under freight cars, the farm worker was more and more apt to travel in a car, accompanied by his family. And this of course created a demand for cheap, temporary housing: in other words, for box houses.

Most of these were probably built by small-time developers or speculators; the only reliable information we have about them is in the contemporary publications of the Department of Labor. Inevitably these box houses for transients were overcrowded, poorly maintained, and dangerous, and one of the programs of the New Deal was to replace them. The problem of course is still with us, but by the 1950s a new form of dwelling, a dwelling strikingly similar in one respect to its medieval forebears, came on the scene: the trailer or mobile home and even more recently the camper on the back of a pickup.

We are only beginning to recognize the impact of this new kind of dwell-ing on planning, on the community, and on work. I am convinced that the trailer or an improved version of it is, for better or worse, the low-cost dwelling of the future—lacking in solidity, lacking in permanence, lacking in charm, but inexpensive, convenient, and mobile.

Most of us, I suspect, find it easier to accept and even romanticize the box house and its American predecessors, at least those in rural areas, that have developed individuality and have been assimilated into the landscape. And yet I persist in seeing an underlying similarity among all those flimsy, short-lived American dwellings, each of which was denounced in its day as crude and disruptive and socially undesirable. All of them have served as dwellings for people who have to move to where the job is: migrant farm laborers, highway and construction crews, lumbermen, soldiers, and airmen. Whatever their form of construction, they have served as dwellings of old people, of young couples getting started in life; and almost always they have been seen by their occupants as temporary: something better and more lasting is to be that next step.

It is very tempting to analyze the dwelling entirely in socioeconomic terms; certainly dwellings do not lend themselves to analysis in terms of architecture or folk art. But the real significance of the temporary dwelling, of the box house, to take one example out of many, lies elsewhere. I think it has always offered, though for a brief time only, a kind of freedom we often undervalue: the freedom from burdensome emotional ties with the environment, freedom from communal responsibilities, freedom from the tyranny of the traditional home and its possessions; the freedom from belonging to a tight knit social order; and above all, the freedom to move on to somewhere else. Now that environmentalism has become accepted Establishment philosophy, the values we stress are stability and permanence and the putting down of roots and holding on to our architectural heritage; and no doubt this is as it should be. Still, we cannot help but be reminded, whenever we look at our rapidly changing landscape and study our changing attitudes toward the home, that we have a second architectural tradition, a tradition of mobility and short-term occupancy that is stronger and more visible than ever. Not everyone can sympathize with this other, more popular tradition with its rejection of environmental loyalties and constraints, but all of us who think about architecture and its many bewildering manifestations are in a sense duty bound to try to understand the new kind of home we are all making in America.

Not everyone is aware that one of the twelve apostles was by way of being an architect. This was Thomas, sometimes called Judas Thomas, the brother of James and the half-brother of Jesus. He described himself as a builder and carpenter. "In wood," he declared, "I can make plows, yokes, ox goads, pulleys, and boats and oars and masts. And in stone: pillars, temples and courthouses for kings."

Because of these talents he was hired by an Indian merchant and taken to India, where he eventually preached the gospel and was martyred. The *Apocryphal Acts of Thomas* tells in passing of his architectural career. The text dates from the third century A.D., so it is a very early account of an architect dealing with a client.

A rich Indian king heard about Thomas and asked if he could build him a palace. Thomas replied that he could. I quote from the narrative.

> And the king took him and went out of the city gates and began to speak with him on the way concerning the building of the courthouse, and of the foundations, how they should be laid, until they came to the place wherein he desired that the building should be; and he said: Here will I that the building should be.
> And the apostle said, yea, for this place is suitable for the building. . . .
> So the King said, Begin to build.
> But he said, I cannot begin now at this season.
> And the king said, when canst thou begin?
> And he said, I will begin in the month of Dius and finish in Xanthicus [which is to say, he would begin in November and finish in April].
> But the king marvelled and said, Every building is builded in summer and canst thou in this very winter build and make ready a palace?

Thomas assured him that he could. The king then asked for a plan. The text continues:

> And the apostle took a reed and drew, measuring the place; and the doors he set toward the sun-rising, to look toward the light—and the windows toward the west to the breezes, and the bakehouse he appointed to be toward the south, and the aqueduct for the service toward the north. And the king saw it and said to the apostle: Verily thou art a craftsman, and it befitteth thee to be a servant of kings. And he left much money with him and departed from him.

According to the narrative, from time to time the king sent more money, and Thomas assured him that he would soon be finished. The text continues:

> When the king came to the city he inquired of his friends concerning the palace . . . and they told him: neither hath he built a palace nor done ought else of what he promised to perform, but he goeth about the cities and countries, and whatsoever he hath he giveth to the poor, and teacheth of a new God, and healeth the sick and driveth out devils and doeth many other wonderful things. . . . And when the king heard that, he rubbed his face with his hands and shook his head for a long space.

105

As might be imagined, Thomas soon found himself in serious trouble. The king had him seized and sentenced him to be flayed alive and then burned. But Thomas was saved. In a miraculous manner it was learned that by distributing the money to the poor and afflicted, Thomas has built the king a splendid palace in heaven, and when this became known, the king exonerated him. It was only many years later that Thomas met his martyrdom.[1]

Even though the palace had only a symbolic existence, we find it easy to visualize, for in many ways it conforms to certain traditional architectural types and procedures. The hollow square—such being the meaning of the term "courthouse for a king"—was a familiar Middle Eastern building type and suggests the Syrian origin of this apocryphal text. The details of the orientation of the palace are admittedly confusing, but I am tempted to read the layout in terms of cosmic symbolism. Like all temples and palaces of the early Christian period and all churches until a much later date, the palace faces the rising sun, or the source of light. The aqueduct perhaps should be interpreted as symbolic of one of the four elements: water; and the bakehouse as symbolic of another element: fire. As for the windows facing the breezes of the west, these could be symbolic of a third element: air. But where is earth, the fourth element? Is it somehow identified with the sacred light coming from the east? Some readers would probably like to think of the location of the aqueduct and the bakehouse as being determined by ecology or convenience, but to me a religious or cosmic symbolism is much more probable. It is hard to imagine an Indian king congratulating his architect on having produced an efficient plan for traffic flow.

If we are to derive any architectural insight from the career of the Apostle Thomas we would have to analyze what he had to say about his craft. He described himself, it will be recalled, as a builder and carpenter. The distinction between the two callings is clear, but Thomas seems to define it less in terms of scale and complexity and importance than in terms of the materials used. He does not put carpentry in an inferior place merely because it involves the making of such items as yokes and plows and boats and oars—and probably chairs and tables; he implies that carpentry involves not merely the production of everyday useful items, but the production of things which eventually wear out and have to be replaced.

On the other hand, Thomas tells us that he used stone for "pillars and temples and courthouses for kings"—an impressive listing, making it evident that he was not only a craftsman, but what we would now call an architect. Stone was a noble material, not just because it was used for noble purposes, noble buildings. It was noble because it had been extracted from the depths of the earth and was timeless.

All this was little enough to go on, and it told nothing about the art of building, whether in wood or stone, that could not have been learned elsewhere. But in a search for insight into the significance of the dwelling we should reject no help, however slight it may appear to be. It was obvious that the palace Thomas was to have built for the king (and which in a sense he *did* actually build in heaven) was to be understood as a symbol; signifying fame or power or a kind of regal presence which would increase or confirm the status of the king. But while there is nothing mysterious in this interpretation, it is interesting—and perhaps significant—that the symbol of power or presence should be a *house*—a palace; and I wonder if one of the attributes of the palace of stone is not some degree of timelessness?

Duration in any case seems to have been a way of classifying buildings. You may object that we no longer classify houses and structures by the length of time they last; and that is true—except that we now seem merely to have shifted our criteria and instead of always preferring long-lasting construction, we tend to choose the material in terms of how long *we* intend the building to last. As Mircea Eliade expresses it, "Modern man takes upon himself the function of temporal duration; in other words, he takes on the role of time."[2]

But this is to anticipate my ideas about the nature of certain types of architecture. Thomas, I think, spoke for an ancient tradition when he classified buildings in terms of the durability of the material used. And (in view of his religious interpretation of that palace) it is likely that he would have defended the distinction between wood and stone by pointing out that many man-made objects in the landscape were meant to last much longer than others; that only a few things in the world were intended to last more than a lifetime; that only things having a sacred character deserved to be carefully designed and made; that in fact most of the objects used in our everyday existence can and indeed *should* be temporary and makeshift and forgettable. All that we ask of our landscape, Thomas would have said, was a monument or two of stone, a series of landmarks to remind us of what we believe and of our origin and identity. Finally that he would have insisted that these landmarks have a permanent, visible character, that they be an integral part of the landscape, part of the cosmic order, and that they have the immediate emotional appeal of a widely recognized archetype.

This viewpoint is foreign to us; yet it is identified with a long and fruitful period in human development—a period which in our part of the world was brought to an end by the teachings of the Renaissance. So it could be worthwhile inquiring into the stone or monumental architecture of Thomas and his innumerable craftsmen colleagues, speculating as to why that architecture fell from favor and seeking to discover what has taken its place.

If one can refer to the masonry work Thomas presumably undertook as architecture one could say that its most prominent feature was its dependence, its relationship to a divine or cosmic prototype, its constant endeavor to reproduce—indeed to become a part of—that divine or cosmic order: an endeavor which was abandoned by architects beginning, shall we say, in the seventeenth century. A brief explanation of how that earlier architecture sought to be part of the divine environment can be found in a book that many readers are probably familiar with. "The intention of the Temple," says Lethaby in his book, *Architecture, Mysticism, and Myth* (and his remarks hold for the church and the palace and the tomb and even for the city), "was to set up a local reduplication—a sort of model to scale, its form governed by the science of the time; it was a heaven, an observatory, and an almanac. Its foundation was a sacred ceremony, the time carefully chosen by augury, and its relation to the heavens defined by observation. Its place was exactly below the Celestial prototype . . . its foundations could not be moved, if they were placed four-square to the walls of the firmament."[3]

The symbolic value of stone resides in far more than its durability and permanence, and it is when we venture into the literature and folklore of stone that we eventually discover its role in pre-Renaissance architecture. The symbolism of stone—and of precious gems—is an essential element in the ritual and belief of many pre-Christian religions and of early Christianity itself. In the primitive view of nature, stone is not dead, it is a concentration of power and life. That is why the touching of sacred stones brings fertility, and according to a widespread custom, sterile women touch sacred stones in order to bear children. Both the Old Testament and the New contain numerous references to stone as the symbol of Jehovah or his presence, and the Apostle Simon was given the name Petros (*stone* in Greek): "Upon this rock will I build my church, and the gates of hell will not prevail against it." Thus the true significance of stone lay not only in its immense age, its slow maturing over the millennia, but in its cosmic, extraterrestrial origin. "The stone parentage of the first men is a theme which occurs in a large number of myths," Eliade tells us. "Deucalion threw the 'bones of his mother' behind his back to repopulate the world. These 'bones' of the Earth-Mother were stones; they represented the *Urgrund,* indestructible reality, life and holiness, the matrix whence a new mankind was to emerge. That the stone is an archetypal image expressing absolute reality, life and holiness is proved by the fact that numerous myths recount the story of gods born from the petra genetrix."[4]

Speculation about the occult realm of stones and gems leads to the exploration of the depths of our own nature. This was understood by those alchemists who, as Jung made clear, investigated the world of rocks and gems and metal and who discovered hidden truths about man. "The sublunary world," Gaston Bachelard remarks, "is divided for the alchemist into three kingdoms: the mineral kingdom, the vegetable kingdom, and the animal kingdom. . . . The rhythm of the animal kingdom is that of everyday existence. The rhythm of the vegetable kingdom is that of the year. The rhythm of the mineral kingdom is that of the ages, of life calculated in millennia. As soon as we contemplate the thousands of years of existence for metals, cosmic dreams come to us."[5] He quotes a German psychologist to the effect that the descent into the depths of the earth, even when it is metaphorical as in poetry or art, is a revealing symbol in the study of the unconscious. Stones, gems, to be understood, must be dreamt about, and whereas the flexibility and adaptability of wood allows us to use it without understanding its basic nature, stone demands that we think of origins.

It is the mysterious power possessed by stone, the manner in which it linked the cosmic order with our own inner search for order that accounts in large part for its architectural importance. "There is very little doubt that during the entire Middle Ages there existed the belief in a distinct relationship between stones and stars."[6] Even those of us not versed in the rich literature of medieval architecture are aware that in the Dark Ages no wood, not even a crucifix of wood, was willingly admitted into churches, and that the early church fathers interpreted the quarrying, the shaping and polishing and putting in place of the stones used in building churches in theological terms. "Today, when the original treatment of the stone has disappeared, we are only occasionally aware of it, chiefly there where old stained glass windows still gleam and where their light transforms the stone. We should think of the Cathedral not only in terms of color, but as being suffused with the atmosphere of light . . . the building should 'shine,' 'sparkle,' 'glitter,' 'dazzle'. . . . It would however be false to say that the Cathedral denies its stone character. It keeps it throughout, only it idealizes it by giving it a gemlike, transfigured, vibrant, crystaline aspect."[7]

Our generation can probably most easily understand the reverence for stone in the medieval church as a form of reverence for the laws governing nature. Indeed, I think that in those pre-Renaissance endeavors to comply with cosmic laws and cosmic relationships—in orientation, proportion, color, and form—we can glimpse a medieval Christian kind of environmentalism. I am no admirer of the contemporary environmental movement, but who cannot be aware of how strong the desire now is to harmonize with nature? We can only hope that in the course of time our present version of environmentalism will acquire some of the piety and vision of the medieval approach.

What Eliade described as "lithic mythology," or the lore and symbolism of stones and gems, underwent a change of direction in the later Middle Ages. Insofar as it was related to the alchemist's search for the philosophers' stone—the elixir basic to all matter—the study of stones and metals shifted from the mystical to the human: to the investigation of the property of substances and their effects on the human body—shifted, in other words, to chemistry and medicine. But even before this development a new theory of architecture had sharply reduced the mystical elements in design and in the use of stone. No longer seen as the symbol of "absolute reality, life and holiness," stone played a more subordinate role in the esthetic quality of the building, interior as well as exterior. It was conspicuous not in its unadorned state, but in the form of

Classical columns and pilasters, elements in a work of art designed to celebrate the human presence and the human scale. In its exterior treatment stone
was made to suggest the passage of historical time: various types of rustica-
tion, the superposition of the several orders, symbolized a social hierarchy
and the evolution of civilization. The historical origin of architecture and of
building materials was debated at length during the seventeenth and eighteenth centuries. Did architecture derive from stone or wood? Giambattista
Piranesi argued that the first man-made structures had been of stone and had
undoubtedly been Egyptian, but Jacques Blondel, in his time the leading
French architectural theoretician, maintained that the Greeks had first built in
wood, then reproduced their wooden buildings in stone. The sanctity of
stone did not enter the discussion.

A final episode in the history of lithic mythology was the emergence in the
seventeenth and eighteenth centuries of a taste for artificial masonry ruins
and even artificial rock formations, and at much the same period geologists
and artists discovered the fascination and beauty of massive rock formations
in mountain scenery or at the edge of the sea. Geologists saw them as the
product of enormous telluric forces and as evidence of the great age of the
earth. Artists and amateurs of the natural landscape admired them as evidence
of nature's inexhaustible creative power. Yet neither the scientific nor the
emotional response revived the sacred interpretations of the remote past, and
the inner composition of rocks and stones, their secret nature, was not investigated. Like the playful ruins produced by architects, stone was a way of
establishing the passage of time in terms comprehensible to rational men.

How are we to interpret the development over the last century of such
man-made substitutes for stone as concrete, reinforced concrete, steel, and
glass in construction? How are they related to the ancient distinction, suggested by St. Thomas, between the enduring landmark and the temporary
wooden or earthen building? The question is not entirely without significance, for as I have suggested, the essential function of any landscape is to
combine the monumental, the landmark, with the transitory.

At first glance these new materials seem to represent the ultimate rejection
of stone as a symbol of timelessness. We have all but entirely broken away
from the Renaissance concept of an architecture standing for permanence and
political power, an architecture of stone celebrating an unchangeable political
and religious order. The notion of building a symbol for posterity—much
less a symbol for the ages—is no longer, except in the case of a few commem-
orative monuments, taken seriously.

Nevertheless, and perhaps without our realizing it, the distinction between
buildings meant to last and buildings meant to be temporary is still part of
our contemporary landscape, and if we do not as yet recognize it that is
because we still think in terms of Renaissance permanence. But while we

seem to have drastically shortened the life span of the building as landmark, we have also shortened the life span of the temporary building—dwelling, place of work, place of recreation. Often unnoted by the architectural historian, who is almost exclusively concerned with public or institutional building, there has emerged over the last century, particularly over the last half century, a vast number of structures designed and built to last for a period measured in a few years if not in months. It is unnecessary to list the new temporary materials, temporary construction techniques, temporary functions which have produced these new fugitive types. It may however be said that they have restored the relationship between the permanent and the temporary in our landscape. If the contrast is no longer between timeless stone and short-lived wattle and mud, or between permanent Renaissance design and wood, the contemporary contrast is potentially just as serviceable: it is the contrast, I believe, between buildings (perhaps of reinforced concrete or of glass and steel) which provide us if not with permanence at least with continuity, as against a mobile, prefabricated, manufactured building of synthetic or plastic materials, buildings deliberately designed to serve a temporary need.

We have yet to learn that we can no longer aspire to permanence in our communities, but merely to their continuity. We cling to old buildings and old urban forms even when they have no artistic or religious or political significance. The restoration of nondescript old houses or old residential neighborhoods is pleasant enough in prosperous communities with a history of their own, but is this the way of providing continuity for communities which are poor or too new to have a history? Whatever we like to think, in hard times (which eventually come to every community no matter what its size or wealth) what makes survival possible and desirable is not its archeological identity but its ability to continue, and it continues because some structures, some institutions and facilities provide continuity. These are the landmarks.

What will these landmarks be? As our dwellings, our places of work or business become increasingly dependent on community services and above all increasingly dependent on institutions devoted to preserving continuity with the past, we will find that we have evolved a whole new series of landmark structures: power plant, bank, hospital, place of public assembly, museum and library and public archives, and not least important, storage warehouse. Whether they are concrete monoliths or not, these stand for continuity, community identity, for links with the past and the future. In the contemporary American community these roles are what counteract our mobility and fragmentation and forgetfulness of history.

Those are not yet inspired specimens of architecture. If we treat them with respect, if we endow them with something like monumentality they will mature and eventually acquire the character of landmarks. What St. Thomas seems to have believed is something that we still believe: that a landscape is not complete or even livable unless it acknowledges and celebrates the role of time and unless it builds monuments to give meaning and dignity to our short existence on earth.

Craftsman Style and Technostyle

Craftsman-style house of the 1920s. (Photo: author)

◄ *Cement house for a city street, with interior view. (From* The Craftsman, *May, 1909)*

There was a period, beginning shortly after the turn of the century and lasting until the mid-twenties, when the American dwelling and particularly the anonymous, mass-produced, middle-class dwelling reflected a fateful change in American culture—specifically a change in our attitude toward the meaning of work.

The traditional attitude that work was undertaken to satisfy basic personal or domestic needs and the need for self-justification assumed its final ideological form in the Arts and Crafts movement in England. Though its inspiration derived from Carlyle and Ruskin, it was under the leadership of William Morris in the 1880s that the movement achieved a semblance of organization. Almost from the start it was linked with parallel movements in France and Central Europe, and it continued to be an important element in the intellectual and artistic climate of the Old World until the eve of World War I.

The Arts and Crafts movement had begun as a form of protest, chiefly among artists and social critics, against the ugliness and injustices of industrial civilization, as well as against the decline of the handicrafts that industrialization had brought about. The decline had had two unhappy results: tastelessness and poor quality in most of the manufactured products and frustration and alienation among the workers. Although many of the leaders of the movement were active in proposing social change and reform, most were concerned with reviving the arts, especially those arts identified with domestic life and the home. Walter Crane, one of the influential figures of the movement in England, believed that the handicrafts were the basis of all art. On this premise his followers undertook to design and make jewelry, pottery, furniture, textiles, and wallpaper. They became interested in typography, stained glass, and dress as well, but architecture was the art, or craft, which they were especially eager to improve. This they hoped to do by seeing that the architect was given the opportunity of expressing his skill and genius in original design and ornamentation instead of his being compelled, as was often the case, to copy and reinterpret old forms, Classical or Gothic.

In the 1890s the movement spread to America. A group was formed in Chicago in 1893, and in 1897 the first American Society of Arts and Crafts was founded in Boston. The American version never achieved the distinction or influence of the English, but it enjoyed for a brief time a wide popularity, and it left a decided mark on the middle-class dwelling and its appearance.

In 1893 Elbert Hubbard established the Roycroft Press in East Aurora, New York. He not only introduced new standards of artistic printing and bookmaking to America, but also effectively publicized the philosophy of the Arts and Crafts movement in his widely read periodicals *The Notebooks, The Philistine,* and *The Fra,* and in his innumerable lectures and essays. East Aurora was, for a time, a place where low-priced furniture and pottery of the Arts and Crafts movement were sold.

Then in 1900 Gustav Stickley, originally a furniture maker, started publishing *The Craftsman*. For eighteen years the magazine offered fresh and stimulating articles on all aspects of art and design, with emphasis on the work of those artists who were part of the movement. Writings by William Morris, Tolstoy, Kropotkin, and Maeterlinck appeared in *The Craftsman,* and during its first decade it was one of the leading journals of social and artistic comment in America. In its pages were to be found intelligent discussions of architecture, landscape architecture, village improvement, and industrial reform. Stickley himself produced many designs for craftsman-style dwellings—an idiom largely of his own devising—suited to the needs and skills of Americans of modest resources. The designs were scarcely inspired, but their emphasis on simplicity and practicality, their picturesque use of fieldstone and shingle, and their unadorned structural elements undoubtedly appealed to many home builders throughout the country. It was Stickley who first called attention to the merits of the California bungalow and helped popularize it in other regions, and it was he who not only produced or designed much of the mission furniture once so much admired, but who rediscovered the Windsor chair.

On a popular level, the American version of the Arts and Crafts movement with its advocacy of democratic reform was largely the creation of Stickley, and it died when *The Craftsman* died. His contributions were criticized by the more knowing among the artists of the time, but it is thanks to his influence that the Arts and Crafts movement in America displayed so large a social ingredient. If some of the esthetic manifestations were inept, the true importance of the movement lay in the new, or revived, dignity it gave to work—work done by hand, by workmen not in the factory but in the home or shop: for the value of this kind of work was not production in the industrial sense, but self-expression and self-justification. No matter how humble he might have been, the craftsman interpreted and gave form to traditional images of universal validity.

This exalted interpretation of work was not shared by the factory worker or by management, but it was endorsed by middle-class Americans and by the academic world. The consequence of the belief was the conviction that the very *process* of work was no less beautiful, no less significant, than the finished article itself. The conviction derived in part from an esthetic reaction against the slick and impersonal aspects of the mass-produced item, but part of it derived from an uneasy social conscience—always a sensitive point among supporters of the movement.

A traditional social order is not concerned with singling out the manual worker for special recognition. After all, everyone has an appointed role to play—farmer, priest, soldier, housewife; why reward the craftsman more than others? Why pay unusual attention to the visible evidence of his having worked? In such a society art is essentially the *concealing* of art, of toil, of process; it seeks to obliterate or cover the mark of the tool with paint or plaster. This is far from being the case, however, in an industrial social order such as ours. Even before the turn of the century there was widespread dissatisfaction with reported working conditions in factories and with the psychological plight of the factory worker. Americans of goodwill felt obligated to take the process of work into account in their appraisal of many products. The handmade article was therefore doubly satisfying: it indicated that the iniquitous factory system had been bypassed, and it offered visible evidence of the process of creation in the mark of the tool.

That no doubt was one reason why, almost from the very beginning of the movement, pottery proved to be the most popular of all the revived handicrafts. Not only—so the belief went—was it preeminently a woman's craft, intimately related to the hearth and the cooking or eating utensil, it was also the immediate product of the hand functioning as a tool; it often displayed the imprint of the potter's palm and fingers. The tendency has always been strong in America to admire manual dexterity and the rough ingenuity of the pioneer or woodsman, and it was easy, once the idea had been endorsed by artists and critics, to appraise almost every creation according to the process by which it had been produced. This was true not merely in works of handicraft but in formal works of art as well. A surface, whether of a piece of handmade furniture, a handwoven rug, or an oil painting, that revealed the mark of the tool or of the hand was almost always revered and understood.

The enthusiasm for hand-produced textures soon extended to the house itself. In early issues of *The Craftsman* much attention is devoted to hand-worked surfaces and the pleasures to be derived from the sense of kinship with nature that comes from the natural textures of wood, leather, and stone worked by the human hand. Many years after the stylistic novelties of the Craftsman movement had ceased to interest Americans, when the mission furniture, the curtains of hand-loomed monks' cloth, the earthenware soup tureens had been relegated to the attic, the obsession with handmade textures was still strong.

Indeed, beginning about 1910 this obsession with the handmade extended to new fields of experience. With the enforced use of such fireproof or fire-retarding building materials as brick, concrete, and stucco, a variety of exterior textures were created. New troweling effects, each with a trade name, each with its own patented trowel, came on the market. Bricks produced in random dimensions with new rough surfaces and new glazes were to be laid with mortar to create carefully irregular bonding patterns and startling surfaces. Stone was artfully inserted in stucco walls, and shingles were manufactured to suggest the handmade, the weathered, the patched. Those architectural idioms, especially popular in the period between the two World Wars—the English cottage, the French farm, the Spanish or Italian casa, the Cape Cod house—can be interpreted, at least in part, as specimens of new exterior textures; half-timbering, imitation thatch, rough masonry, exposed beams, and hand-hewn shingles.

We are still inclined to dismiss these fashions as indicating little more than the romanticism of the middle-class American home owner, and an element of romanticism was certainly there. But what we should not overlook is the redefinition, on the popular level, of style in domestic architecture. At a time when prominent American architects were still thinking and designing within traditional academic idioms, and in fact taking pride in historical accuracy, the relatively obscure designer of the middle-class dwelling was producing styles defined by workers and techniques of work. Vastly enlarged, hopelessly inaccurate in detail, entirely up-to-date in utilities and plan, these dwellings recalled not a traditional period as such but traditional manual occupations. They were the modern versions of the homes of the fisherman, farmer, craftsman, and colonial pioneer.

Writing in 1929, Talbot Hamlin, a popular critic of the times, mentioned this fascination with surface textures as one of the characteristics of American domestic architecture of the period. He complained that architects and deco-rators—and presumably consumers—were so infatuated with old-fashioned, antiqued textures that they failed to appreciate the beauty of some of the new synthetic building materials and disguised them to resemble weathered wood, stone masonry, or hand-troweled plaster.

Such criticism did not put an end to this vestigial Craftsman style. What accomplished that was the gradual shift in attitudes toward work, a growing awareness of the predominance of industrial methods in almost every aspect of the economy. Work on the part of the individual, whether in an office, a factory, or a school, was more and more identified with organized mass production and efficiency. The dwelling itself, as new materials, new work methods, and increased standardization were introduced, became a vivid demonstration of work as a form of industrial production. When more and more of the picturesque features were mass-produced, even the ghost of the traditional craftsman vanished from sight.

Paradoxically, Stickley contributed to the decline of the traditional philos-ophy of work. In his desire to provide as wide a public as possible with the benefits of craftman simplicity and reasonable cost, he advocated, early in the movement, the use of machinery and modern work procedures. In 1906 he declared in *The Craftsman,* "The invention of modern machinery is in itself a notable advancement of the true spirit of craftsmanship. . . . When rightly used, the machine is simply a tool in the hands of a skilled worker, and in no way detracts from the quality of his work." Frank Lloyd Wright expressed the same acceptance of the machine a year later, though for a different reason, but both men were in strong disagreement with the prevailing crafts philosophy. In 1900 it was still realistic for an architect to feel the need to go back to the status of an actual workman in order to be able to advance his work to the status of real architecture. Yet by the mid 1930s, if not earlier, the last traces of the craftsman work philosophy seem to have vanished. A new kind of dwelling keyed to a new philosophy of work—work as a means of production—had been accepted by the average American. It is still with us today.

The new philosophy of work derived in large part from the principles of scientific management formulated in 1911 by Frederick Winslow Taylor. Originally inspired by a determination to introduce mechanical efficiency and greater production into the American factory, it emphasized standardization of work methods, tools, and parts, assembly-line techniques, division of labor into small, highly specialized tasks, and the greatest possible degree of mechanical precision in the manufacturing process. Time-and-motion studies, new methods of training, supervision, and production planning eventually transformed not only the role of the worker but the environment of the factory as well.

The remarkable achievements of scientific management were not long in being recognized. The principles were applied in offices, government agencies, and many types of business enterprise. The cafeteria, which made its first appearance in Chicago in 1907, was a conspicuous example of the new scientific efficiency, and in fact the decline of the boarding house beginning at the turn of the century has been partly ascribed to the advent of scientific management with its higher standards of cleanliness and efficiency in restaurants. In *Mechanization Takes Command*, Siegfried Giedion has described how Taylor's principles led to the transformation of the American kitchen and bathroom. The new discipline of home economics or domestic science derived from the same source, and during the first decades of the twentieth century it was widely assumed that the American home would soon be radically redesigned in accord with the principles of scientific management to become (according to one proponent of the new work philosophy) a factory under the management of the housewife for the production of young citizens.

Still, if emphasis on efficiency had been the only effect of Taylorism on the American home, we would be justified in dismissing it as a temporary fashion, soon forgotten. Efficiency, tidiness, and avoidance of waste are not characteristic of the American household now, and probably never were, even in the heyday of Taylor's prestige. Scientific management came to the fore once again at a later date and in much more sophisticated guise.

In the beginning it had merely undertaken to organize and systematize work. That first mechanically oriented phase lasted unchallenged in many factories for perhaps two decades and assumed its most spectacular form in the moving assembly line in Detroit in 1913. But it became evident in many factories managed according to Taylor's principles that workers were increasingly dissatisfied with the emphasis on mechanical efficiency and the neglect of psychological and physical needs. Management soon realized that the machine and the task assigned to the worker should be adjusted to his or her limitations, that the social and physical environment within the factory had to improve.

Who was to undertake the reforms? Clearly not the engineer alone. It was a job calling for the combined skills of the sociologist, the psychologist, the artist, and even, on occasion, the physician. There is a variety of terms for the study, which often included the school and the hospital and their respective occupants. All derive from the early attempts of scientific management to justify its philosophy of work. They have been variously known as "human engineering," "psychophysics," and "space planning." Attempts to improve the work environment of the office are known as "office landscaping" or even "environotics."

Professionals in the new environmental discipline set to work to make the factory more agreeable and more efficient. Many machines were redesigned to lessen strain. More short breaks in the workday were introduced. After appropriate study, better lighting was installed. Cleanliness and hygiene in the factory were emphasized, and a standard color code was introduced to convey information and warnings: yellow, be careful; orange, danger; red, protection against fire; green, safety; and so on. Work spaces and installations were relocated to promote safety and to improve traffic flow. Noise levels were reduced and excessive temperatures moderated.

All of these changes were designed to improve the physical environment, the conditions under which men and women were compelled to work, but there were also attempts to create better psychological environments, to create a mood of contentment in order to encourage steady attention to the job. In this area the light-and-color psychologist played an important role. Faber Birren, the best known of American color experts, has defined his work in these terms:

> I have studied the elusive properties of color harmony and human emotion, striving to find new relationships between color and form, between the physical reality of color and the strange reactions that seem to arise from it. . . . I have written color plans and specifications for industrial plants, office buildings, hospitals, schools, stores, and commercial establishments. . . . My endeavor . . . has centered around an attempt to find new values for color to aid human efficiency and well-being, to contribute to human comfort and to control human moods.[1]

The use of color for psychological as well as decorative and informational purposes inevitably introduced a new element into industrial environmental design. To be effective in work surroundings color must have its own kind of lighting and its own kind of surfaces—clean, simple surfaces capable of reflecting light. Artificial illumination usually means the exclusion of daylight, so the factory environment tends to be totally artificial and self-contained, almost entirely detached from the surrounding building. Since the contemporary factory is usually planned with expansion in mind, or perhaps for an entirely different kind of operation sometime in the future, there is no real attempt to reconcile temporary function and permanent form. The building serves as an envelope, a loose-fitting packaging whose exterior is designed not to indicate the process going on within but to impress the outsider.

Color, therefore, plays a unique and important role: it is not merely decoration, it is atmosphere, and precisely because of its importance, most responsible color-psychologists insist that it have a calming effect. Light green, the color that has invaded almost all our public institutions, was first adopted as a suitable background color for factories because it was held to be restful and soothing.

A familiar instance of environmental engineering is the experiment conducted in the Hawthorne plant of Western Electric during the 1920s. It was started by engineers who wanted to learn what the effects of different kinds of lighting would be on the output of workers. Before the experiment came to an end nine years later, it had involved not only lighting, but color, temperature, humidity, and noise. The fact that none of the changes had much effect on the production did not discourage other attempts along the same line. The point is that, beginning more than a half-century ago, when the modern movement in architecture and design had not been heard of by the average American, there evolved in a very inauspicious setting a coherent system of environmental design. It was sparked not by any dissatisfaction with the artistic status quo but simply by a desire to produce an efficient and agreeable environment for work. In countless factories, schools, hospitals, and stores built during the first third of the century we discover most of the ingredients of the style still popular in many American homes: color to produce moods; smooth and uniform surfaces of glass, plastic, and aluminum; open spaces; light used to create a totally autonomous interior and environment; and emphasis on horizontal layout for efficiency's sake. Above all, the exterior of the house is designed as a colorful package that conceals the content, which is privacy.

A combination of circumstances made this vernacular style recognizable and acceptable. The influence of the Paris Exposition of 1926, though late in being felt, opened the eyes of many of the merits of their local commercial and industrial esthetic. Far more significant than the influence of the exposition, however, was the growing familiarity of countless thousands of employees in office, factory, and store with the attractions of effective lighting; clear, bright colors; and uncluttered spaces. Until the Depression, the housing industry continued to introduce new industrialized methods and new building materials very much in keeping with the new taste. Speed and lightness were seen as basic ingredients of the emerging American idiom, and the new materials suggested that walls, exterior as well as interior, reject their traditional weight-bearing function and serve merely as an epidermis. Masonry was no longer to be used; in its place were to be found the new veneer materials, products of the machine, not the craftsman.

Mass production of dwellings presented the industry with the problem of monotony. The industry solved it as long ago as 1920 by introducing color psychology: brightly painted houses carefully interspersed among houses painted in softer colors gave the illusion of spatial variety. Color, in fact, was to be the keynote of the Chicago Century of Progress Fair—colors and the flat, impersonal textures which best reflect them. The display of model homes, called Design for Living, included houses built of Masonite, Rostone, Ferro-enamel, and Stran-Steel. The essentially traditional nature of the one house built of wood was somewhat disguised by its designation as a creation of the lumber industry. Though far from having been an artistic event of note, the Century of Progress Fair did publicize three significant innovations in domestic architecture: the garage became an integral part of the facade of the dwelling; the chimney, totally divorced from cooking and heating, became the symbol of domestic leisure in the living room; and the cellar was eliminated in favor of the concrete slab, thereby increasing the horizontality of the dwelling's layout.

We are not accustomed to thinking of a new architectural idiom making its appearance in the *interior* of a building. A change of plan or of construction methods is what we usually look for. But the American technostyle of the 1930s got its start inside rather than outside the house. The reason is clear: the Depression had greatly reduced the number of new low-cost houses. All that most families could do was remodel. So it was the interior decorator, the color consultant, the experts in the family magazines and Sunday supplements, and not the architect, who defined and fostered technostyle for the great majority of Americans. Technostyle achieved its acceptance by means of mock-up displays in department stores, in those same windows which were later to inspire the picture windows in the postwar dwelling. Industry devised it, merchandising propagated it, and advertising established the canons of correctness. The style was the creation of a uniquely twentieth-century figure: the behavioral engineer.

Technostyle, like the place of work or business itself, has rejected one by one the traditional spaces within the building. The nomenclature of the dwelling now imitates the nomenclature of the factory: work space, utility space, family space, unloading point, traffic flow. Color psychology, not tradition or taste, tells us how to set the table, how to paint the walls, how to produce an atmosphere of domestic relaxation and fun. Faber Birren, for example, recommends that "color should be emotionally suited to human personality . . . conservative persons (inwardly integrated) have a natural predilection for tradition and sentiment in decoration and for soft, subdued hues, preferably cool. More dynamic souls (outwardly integrated) can appreciate modern, abstract, and more radical design, and with it a bolder array of sharp hues and color contrasts."

Detached from the place of work, detached from neighbors and community, even detached from its architectural exterior, the technostyle home aspires to be an island of leisure and informal relaxation. The man's work—in theory at least—is relegated to the garage, the woman's, to the kitchen; all else is bright surfaces, bright lights, and bright color—behavioral art. In the 1930s the purpose of this art was to arouse a definite mood, and the desirable mood was remoteness from the structured world outside.

This whole environment represents a triumph of the psychological version of Taylor's philosophy of work: a job will be done better and will seem easier when the environment is properly engineered and when that environment can be quickly changed. The American family rejected the traditional home with its traditional values only to fall victim to another set of restraints: mass production, constant change, and hidden persuasion.

Is the new way of living so much worse than the old? Middle-class liberal America pictures the contemporary work environment, whether in office, factory, or commercial establishment, as oppressive and frustrating. What we often ignore is the far more rigid repression of the traditional working home. Cottage industries and the old-fashioned farm represented, especially to the young, the tyranny of tradition and of a meager, colorless, unchanging way of life, and to them the factory offered not only freedom but a new and more stimulating environment. That environment has now been duplicated in many ways in the contemporary home, and for the new American family it is proving satisfactory. In time it will doubtless change. But it will change not in accordance with traditional notions of architectural evolution but in accordance with changes in our philosophy of work and leisure.

BMX track, Wilton, Connecticut. (Photo: Tobé Saskor)

Once cherished by citizens as a public work of art, source of wholesome pleasure, glimpse of unspoiled nature; admired as the democratic equivalent of the royal garden, the American city park, after little more than a century, has lately fallen on evil days. We no longer love it as we did. The prosperous neighborhoods the park did so much to foster now see its presence as a social and economic liability, and its design, its use, its very existence have all become matters of angry debate. How many crestfallen designers there must be! And crestfallen recreationists and social counselors and administrators who find themselves having to reappraise their respective philosophies and come up with fresh and very different justifications for their work.

I hope they start by reexamining their ideas about the origins of the public park, retracing its genealogy. If they do they will discover that they have ignored the oldest and most popular kind of play space in favor of the aristocratic garden.

The current interpretation of the history of the park is neatly expressed in the article "Park and Playground" in the *Encyclopaedia Britannica*—an article, incidentally, written by a playground expert and in its way a gem of misinformation. "The first parks were grants of the royal lands for the enjoyment of the people," it says; "modern parks are gifts from the people to themselves." The role of the royal park or garden was *in fact* briefly as follows: the first designed parks dating from the sixteenth century were formal and elaborate gardens with small wooded areas created and set aside for the delectation of the court, though on occasion open to a limited element of the public. Early royal parks or gardens were extremely formal, even architectural in design, emphasizing what recreationists deprecatingly call passive enjoyment, but it was the so-called picturesque landscape park, the product of eighteenth- and nineteenth-century England, that inspired the design of the public park in America and Europe. The works of Strauch and Downing and Bushnell and Olmsted were essentially modern versions of the private English country estate laid out as a "picturesque" landscape: a composition of lawns, placid bodies of water, artfully located groves of trees, a would-be natural topography affording occasional glimpses of the wider environment. We know that; but we sometimes forget that this particular kind of park was designed to provide contact with nature, that it was expensive to lay out and maintain, that it too produced "passive enjoyment," and that as a work of art it had to be treated with respectful care; correct behavior was essential. In other words, the landscaped park, despite its apparent informality, called for a public which was aware of the esthetic features of the design, was in search of a contact with nature, and was socially disciplined.

When Olmsted and his contemporaries both here and abroad produced the first large city parks they naturally planned in terms of those restraints. The "picturesque," natural beauty of the composition was emphasized, the rural, almost pastoral character carefully maintained, and a code of public de-

127

meanor strictly enforced—as indeed it still is in many European city parks. Contemporary critics of Olmsted like to attack his social philosophy. Robert Moses, for instance, refers to him as "an aristocratic Versailles estate land-scaper, a notorious WASP in his social sympathies." It is a pointless accusa-tion. Central Park from its first years was used by all classes. Early observers noted with pleased surprise that numbers of working-class citizens—"the poor seamstress and journeyman"—were there, along with the rich and powerful.

Why were they surprised? Not because they thought that the poor were out of place in Central Park—though that is what the class-conscious park reformer would like to think—but because they believed, with some justifica-tion, that there were other places for recreation that the poor might well prefer.

And in fact there were. Mid-nineteenth-century New York still contained areas offering a much livelier, a much less formal kind of entertainment, and a much less structured environment. Staten Island was a popular resort, and so were the Elysian Fields in Hoboken; and there were other locations, un-touched by the garden architect, along the beaches and waterfronts and in the unbuilt areas in Manhattan. When the nineteenth-century park enthusiast praised the upper-class aspect of the city park he did so because he assumed the existence and availability of other kinds of recreation.

That is to say, he was aware of something which the contemporary park expert and recreationist has conveniently forgotten: that well into the nine-teenth century every community, large or small, in Europe as well as Amer-ica, retained sizeable areas of land where the common people, and particularly adolescents, could exercise and play and enjoy themselves, and at the same time participate in community life.

The existence of these playgrounds is vouched for by history as well as by tradition. Folklorists find evidence in village after village that a portion of the churchyard and the site of any pre-Christian shrine or temple were commonly identified with youthful sport and games. Some historians suggest that the association between games and places having a traditional sacred character derives from a remote period when the young men of the village were as-signed to guard those sites and fight off neighboring invaders. By the Middle Ages the convention was well established: certain spots, usually near the church, were informally set aside for sports and games. But that is not all: these sports and games, deriving as they did from armed conflict with out-siders, retained a violent, competitive nature, were based on notions of ter-ritoriality and community status, and were little concerned with the design of the terrain in question or with "contact with nature." The games were rough and undisciplined, constantly denounced by the Church and the Crown; but quite evidently very popular among adolescents as a way of "defending" the community, letting off steam, and achieving personal renown.

Nor were such areas and such sports confined to the village. Every medieval town possessed stretches of land outside the walls, often along the banks of a river, where young or active townspeople could enjoy themselves—what the French call *terrains vagues*—pieces of land not cultivated or built upon. Francis I set aside a stretch of river bank in Paris for the recreation of university students, and in 1222, so we read, the young citizens of London "kept games of defense and wrestling near unto the Hospital of St. Giles in the Field, where they challenged and had the mastery of men in the suburbs and other commoners."

New Englanders, despite the disapproval of the Puritan clergy, hunted, fished, played football on the beach, competed in violent sports with neighboring villages, and even frolicked on the common. As for the southern passion for nonestablishment competitive sports, either in the backyard of taverns or along the road in the open country, there is ample historical evidence of its existence.

The advent of the park movement in the second half of the nineteenth century produced innumerable designed parks in towns and cities throughout the United States, but the popularity of the unstructured playground and of unstructured competitive sports persisted. Baseball in its less formal guise, football as a kind of mass confrontation, rodeos, mock war games took place not in the town park but in the so-called grove outside. The landscape architect F. A. Waugh wrote an attractive description in 1889 of the contrast between the formal, overstructured, small-town park, deserted and forlorn, and the much used grove out in the country near the river.

> I have in mind one particular western village of more than usual culture and enterprise. . . . This town has expended many hundreds of dollars in making a park on forty acres of valuable land. One corner is always kept mowed for a baseball field, and this is the extent of the uses found for the park. Quite as near the town, on the opposite side, are uncommonly fine stretches of natural timber, a beautiful river, suitable for boating and bathing, some hills and ravines, which would make a delightful park. These woods, used otherwise only for pasture, constitute The Grove; and to them comes the crowd for the soldiers' reunion, the picnic, the circus, and so forth. . . . The existence of the park shows the public spirit and liberality of the citizens. The general favor in which the grove is held demonstrates the unspoiled instinct for sylvan pleasures.[1]

Why have we so completely forgotten this once popular and lively tradition? Why have our parks ignored this important social function: the integration of the young into the life of the community? For one thing, the grove (as the American equivalent of the *terrain vague*) has vanished from the American scene. The expansion of towns and cities has obliterated it and covered it with houses and streets, and tastes in recreation have radically changed. But current philosophies of recreation and park design are also to blame. The persistence of the belief that what the public wants (or ought to have) is "contact with nature" in a professionally designed park, that sport is exclusively a matter of teams and rules and expertise has meant the elimination of ad hoc playgrounds for adolescents and the public disapproval of any display of risk or competitiveness: twin nightmares that haunt the liberal social reformer.

And in the meantime the older city parks have become the victims of reduced budgets, deteriorated neighborhoods, persistent vandalism. They are misused by undesirable and even dangerous elements, and as a consequence less and less used by those who need them. The value of parks is potentially as great as ever. The formal, structured park or garden, the park as work or art for passive enjoyment is essential as an urban amenity, particularly in the downtown, working area. The less elaborate, more "natural" neighborhood park has a valuable role to play in the lives of those who need contact with nature and in the lives of older people and children. But is it not time that we acknowledged the need for a third variety: the ample, unstructured, unbeautiful, multipurpose public playground where adolescents can assert themselves and become social beings, defending and serving some youthful concept of the community?

The question is by no means idle; there are in fact signs, still inconspicuous, that we are beginning to try to answer it. Many western cities, plagued by the misbehavior of a restless and mobile younger generation, are creating sports parks. Parks, that is to say, which are designed for sports of mobility: bicycling, skateboarding, motorcycling, all-terrain vehicles, and even in some cases for skiing and hang gliding. They are expensive, unsightly, and still in the experimental stage. Anything more unlike the conventional park it would be hard to imagine: noisy, deliberately artificial in its man-made topography, used by a boisterous and undisciplined public, and dedicated to the violent expenditure of energy and to hitherto unheard of contacts with nature, the sports park seems to repudiate and make a mockery of everything the word *park* has stood for. On the other hand, it may eventually mature and give the word a wider and more contemporary meaning: the park as a public, open-air space where we can acquire self-awareness as members of society and awareness of our private relationship to the natural environment.

Siège d'Ypres, *1677*. *(Courtesy Bibliothèque Nationale)*

I am happy to pay my respects to the two groups whose authority and guidance I have always willingly recognized: the professional geographers of this country and the general officers of the United States Army. There was a time when I would have included officers of field grade; but when I became a major myself, I was less impressed with their collective wisdom.

These two groups have taught me what little I know about landscape reconnaissance. I was first exposed to geography under Derwent Whittlesey at Harvard many years ago; and when I was a second lieutenant in 1941, I was sent to an army intelligence school which no longer exists—the Military Intelligence Training Center at Camp Ritchie, Maryland. I believe I was the first trainee to check in at that strange institution.

I learned a good deal while I was there; and when I was at length graduated, I knew everything about the current German order of battle, the organization of the German Army from corps to platoon, the caliber of its various weapons, and how to read or decipher a German *Soldbuch,* as well as all the insignia of rank and branch of service. We also learned map reading.

All this training was presumably to teach us how to collect, evaluate, and disseminate information about the enemy and his capabilities. We did not speculate about the environment and its psychological impact nor about the relationship between the environment and man. The kind of knowledge we acquired was entirely practical and military. We learned to assume that the occupants of that environment were animated by one very clear purpose: to hold on to it as long as they could. We learned to study the environment only insofar as it might help or hinder the carrying out of that purpose. One reason it was easy to ignore the environment was that it was all too familiar. While the make-believe tactical situations were constantly changed, the terrain was always the same fragment of the Blue Ridge Mountains.

In other words, we came to think of the environment as a kind of setting or empty stage upon which certain alarming and unpredictable decisions and actions took place. Geographically speaking, I suppose military intelligence in those far-off days was a very anthropocentric discipline. But so was much geography.

After six months at Camp Ritchie, I was sent to North Africa, where I joined the G-2 section of the 9th Infantry Division; and when we had finished in Tunisia, we were sent to invade Sicily. In both places I had a chance to display my erudition about the makeup of the Hermann Goering Division, the range of the 88 on the modified Tiger tanks, and the shoulder patch of a warrant officer in the quartermaster reserves. I was mortified to see how little difference this information made, but the earlier illusion that environmental factors could be ignored persisted. Both in Africa and in Sicily, we were dealing with fast-moving units racing across a dry and relatively empty landscape. Their impact on the terrain, except for an occasional burst of artillery, was slight. The stage continued to be vacant and uninteresting except when some military action was taking place.

Normandy of course was a different matter, a much more complex and much more familiar landscape. It was when the division headquarters was billeted in a Norman chateau that I discovered a sizeable library devoted to the bocage country—something I had never heard of before, though we were in the midst of it and having trouble getting out of it. It was even possible to buy books by some of the French human geographers—Deffontaines and Vidal de La Blache and Demangeon. This was at a time when G-2 had nothing to do except prophesy the imminent collapse of the German Army.

As we know, it did not collapse in August of 1944, and the 9th Infantry Division and many other divisions passed a cold and uncomfortable winter in the Huertgen Forest. I still don't know why we stayed as long as we did; and like everyone else, I was so sure that in a day or two we would push ahead and capture Cologne and cross the Rhine that all I could think about was the landscape which lay immediately in front of us and which we were convinced we would occupy by the end of the week.

It was a desolate countryside, badly damaged by incessant artillery fire. Nevertheless, it was possible to collect out of the ruins a respectable number of guidebooks, picture postcards, tourist maps, and elementary local geography and history texts; and so for the first time, I began to learn something about a landscape. But again it was almost entirely in human terms, in military terms: How was the enemy using the terrain? how were they exploiting it? where were their installations? and how could we use it once it was ours? This meant studying that tourist literature, examining the picture postcards and textbooks in order to visualize the landscape. If the farmers raised wheat (as some of them did), would our half-tracks bog down in the naked winter fields? Were there roads in the valleys, where there was a problem of bridges, or on the hilltops, where there was a problem of visibility? And the house types had to be identified, so I thought, because I wanted to know if the barns were large enough to accommodate trucks and whether there were orchards where guns could be concealed.

I enjoyed investigating these matters, and I remember the many nights I spent interrogating the few prisoners we got in order to acquire more detailed information about those villages and countrysides and forests. I read the prisoners' diaries, written in indelible pencil under God knows what circumstances, and dutifully examined their *Soldbücher*. I asked them about specific bridges and roads, how they had arrived at their unit, and where the antiaircraft batteries were located; and I finished the questioning by telling them to indicate all these locations on a map. Actually I knew far more about the terrain than they did because most of them had come from a replacement center only a day or two before.

In the morning I always made a detailed report to the general and his chief of staff (who was a handsome, pink-cheeked young colonel from West Point by the name of Westmoreland). While I talked, the general slept, and no doubt dreamt of getting a transfer to an office job in London or Paris.

Eventually my illusion that anyone was interested in the intelligence I had collected and evaluated vanished, and I realized that whenever we *did* advance it would only be after a saturation bombing which would obliterate roads and fields and forests and house types and settlement patterns as if they had never existed. But an illusion of another sort took its place: a private image of the world, or at least of that dark and mysterious landscape ahead of us.

By day I was well aware of its ruins and destruction and of the winter misery surrounding us; but by night, when I was working on the G-2 report, I was transported into an entirely different landscape—a Classical landscape of well-defined places and well-defined inhabitants, all animated by that one collective purpose. The landscape came into being as a result of those innumerable tactical questions: Where are your headquarters? Who is your commanding officer? What is your unit and branch of service? What are the boundaries, the routes, the channels of communication? Even when this landscape trembled from an artillery barrage and burst into flames, I still saw it in my mind's eye as orderly and intelligent, with its clear-cut hierarchy of officers and men, each with his insignia of rank, each one doing a particular duty and filling out a daily report, each one moving through a spatial organization indicated by signs and boundaries. Finally the landscape ceased to be an empty impersonal stage and became part of a whole way of life, a place where men and environment were in harmony with one another and where an overall design was manifest in every detail.

What I had unwittingly reconstructed was a traditional European landscape of the eighteenth century. At the same time it was also a military landscape in every feature. Because I think that the two—at least on the Continent—were in many respects identical, just as the organization of the military and civil societies was in many respects identical. And I still find myself wondering if there is not always some deep similarity between the way war organizes space and movement and the way the contemporary society organizes them; that is, if the military landscape and military society are not both in essence intensified versions of the peacetime landscape, intensified and vitalized by one overriding purpose which, of necessity, brings about a closer relationship between man and environment and between men.

My obsession with this version of landscape was increased by a book I read that winter. It was a popular life of Frederick the Great, distributed, I suppose, by some German book-of-the-month club and found in every middle-class home in the Huertgen Forest. What impressed me was the description of Frederick as an old man, through with war, traveling about his impoverished and ruined country in a carriage, stopping to talk to villagers and farmers. "How much do you pay for bread?" "What rent do you pay?" "What crop are you planting?" Then he would write in a notebook: "Roads very bad in such and such a village; speak to Baron X" or "The mayor is lazy and dishonest; see about having him replaced." What he was collecting was intelligence of an almost Classical sort: What men *did* was what mattered, not what they thought or felt; what the countryside provided in the way of food and shelter was what interested him, not its beauty or its barrenness.

I began to see that regimented landscape in front of us as a kind of formal eighteenth-century garden, and the eighteenth-century formal garden as the regimented militarized state in miniature.

When we finally broke out of the Huertgen Forest in February and rushed ahead to cross the Rhine, I was not entirely happy to see that imaginary landscape disintegrate. Clear-cut identities became blurred; well-established units dissolved into scattered individuals hiding in the woods; boundaries and demarcations ceased to mean anything. And the various headquarters and command posts we had so carefully marked on the acetate overlay proved to be nothing more than heaps of rainsoaked ruins littered with mimeographed orders that no one had bothered to obey or even to read.

The end of the war saw the end of this particular illusion. But I think the experience in the Huertgen Forest taught me something which has no geographical or military value but which has helped me see and enjoy the world: *Every landscape of any size or age has a style of its own, a period style such as we discern or try to discern in music or architecture or painting, and a landscape true to its style, containing enough of the diagnostic traits, whether it is in Appalachia or Southern California, can give an almost esthetic satisfaction.* By accepting this admittedly superficial approach, we can, I think, learn to define other unknown landscapes, provided we know the necessary traits.

I am thinking in particular of the American landscape which has come into existence since my time in the army, almost a half century ago. I cannot truthfully say that my own efforts to understand and appreciate the period qualities of Flatbush or Las Vegas have been very successful. This well may be a matter of age. But it may also be a matter of perspective—whether we see it from the ground or from the air. And this is where I think new intelligence techniques will eventually teach us how to define landscapes, just as they have in the past.

I suspect that the time is not far off, if indeed it has not already arrived, when we will refer to World War II as the last of the classic wars. And one good reason for so doing would be this matter of military intelligence techniques: the manner in which we perceive and evaluate environmental factors. In World War II, G-2 was still almost totally dependent on the ordinance map for its information about the terrain. The vertical aerial photograph was of course widely used; but it was in a sense a photographic transcription of the human eye—more accurate, much more detailed, but still a kind of instant map. It was about thirty years ago that aerial or space photography evolved its own perspective, its own vision. The accomplishments of this new photography are quite beyond my understanding. However, I realize, like everyone else, that it has not only revealed the world to us from a remote point in space but has revealed aspects of the world that entirely transcend the human visual experience; remote sensing and hyperaltitude photography present an image we can only begin to understand after exhaustive interpretation.

But this is no doubt already an accepted preliminary to the acquisition of information—we have to learn to read instead of merely learning to see. And once we have learned to read the new photography, we will discover a new environment and a new relationship between that environment and man and, I dare say, discover a new definition of man. That is what many geographers are trying to do, though again the new techniques in the discipline entirely escape me.

What we do with this insight from outer space remains to be seen. I like to think that in the future some young intelligence officer, puzzling over all this airborne information and trying to evaluate it and disseminate it according to the book, will suddenly glimpse within it a new landscape of harmony and order for the world to aspire to. But for *his* sake, and for the sake of all of us, let us hope that the moment of wartime revelation lies far in the future.

Irrigated fields, southwest U.S. (From Georg Gerster, Flights of Discovery, *London, 1978)*

The best place to find new landscapes is in the West. Pictures painted on canvas is not what I mean, nor glimpses of pleasant rural scenery, but landscapes as we are now learning to see them: large-scale organizations of man-made spaces, usually in the open country.

Spaces of this sort are common everywhere, but it is in the West that they have been given unusual forms and dimensions: compositions of fields hard to interpret when seen at eye-level as we pass through them, but clear and sharply defined when seen from the air; and it is when we fly over it that we begin to understand the American landscape from a new perspective.

I am thinking in particular of the mosaics of irrigated land we so often fly over when traveling from East to West. They are of two kinds: those we see in Nevada and Utah and Arizona stand out in vivid contrast to their pale and empty background of desert, whereas those we see when we are above parts of eastern Washington or west Texas or Colorado or Nebraska have a far less dramatic setting; they seem gradually to emerge out of the rolling prairie. To me these latter irrigated landscapes are the ones especially worth our attention.

Irrigation is of course no novelty in the West. Many irrigated landscapes have flourished here for more than a century, and some, like those in the San Joaquin and Imperial valleys, are rich and vast. Only within the last generation, however, have we been able to see them at a glance from several thousand feet in the air and to perceive them as units; for the first time we were aware of their brilliant variety of color and texture and shape. We fell into the lazy habit of comparing these landscapes to some familiar pattern: to a tapestry or a floor covering or to the work of some painter: Mondrian or Fernand Léger or Diebenkorn. We did not think about what lay beneath the surface; that was not part of the composition as we saw it, and if we speculated about the origin of these landscapes and their ultimate meaning, it was to note the obvious: the miracle of water diverted from a lake or impounded river radically transforming the desert. We saw the enormous dams, the network of ditches, and pondered the organization of men and machines that had produced this miracle. But by then we had left the landscape far behind.

We traveled too fast, and still travel too fast for fresh thinking about what we see below. But flying over that other kind of High Plains irrigated landscape proves to be a different experience. It is so huge and yet so simple in composition that we can study it as we look down, perceive it in other than painterly terms. We no longer see the surface as concealing what is beneath it, but as explaining it.

Only about three decades ago did this new kind of irrigated landscape begin to evolve, and not in the desert but in the rangeland of the High Plains—a region somewhat removed from the main routes of transcontinental air travel, which is perhaps why it has long remained unnoticed. Its most conspicuous feature is the great number of perfectly circular green fields.

141

Almost completely devoid of familiar human installations—houses and roads and towns and groves of trees—this landscape is hard for the eye to measure, but each of these round fields contains 130 acres and is enclosed in a square each of whose sides is a quarter mile long. In parts of the High Plains these round fields seem to stretch without interruption in uniform rows almost to the horizon. Interspersed among them are many large fields which are severely rectangular, some of them long and narrow, others square. No details, natural or man-made, interrupt the expanse of simple geometrical forms. The few roads and highways conform to the overall grid pattern. There is a predominance of shades of green. The landscape is one of extraordinary simplicity and enormous size, but because of its monotony it is best experienced briefly and from the air.

The High Plains is an open, undulating region east of the Rockies, extending from the Canadian border down into west Texas. Sparsely inhabited and with few towns and an inconspicuous scattering of farms and ranches, it once was largely devoted to the raising of wheat and cattle, and it is still a sunlit countryside of cloudless skies and of waving wheat and prairie grass. Rainfall is barely sufficient for farming, and there are few streams for irrigation. But beneath the surface there is a large supply of water, and thanks to new engineering and agricultural techniques and the former availability of cheap energy, this supply has been tapped and brought to the surface for irrigation, and these round fields are the result. There are more than 10,000 of them in western Nebraska, and in west Texas and parts of Colorado and Kansas, even more.

What distinguishes this new irrigated landscape from the older ones, as well as what gives it its circular form, is the fact that the fields are watered not by a ditch or system of dams and ditches leading from some lake or reservoir. Each field has its own central well. A motor, located at the wellhead, drives a perforated aluminum pipe on wheels, a pipe a quarter of a mile long, around the field. Water is dispensed in a uniform spray as the pipe moves at any speed between one revolution a week or one revolution an hour. Mixed with the water thus distributed is often a determined amount of chemical fertilizer, herbicide, or insecticide. Airborne infrared scanners record the ground temperature at any given time, as well as the rate of evaporation, and an appropriate irrigation schedule can be established. For these procedures to be effective and profitable, the precise composition of the soil and of the water has to be known, and the vagaries of the climate studied and taken into account. As for the crops themselves—corn or alfalfa or cotton or sorghum or wheat—genetic engineering is seeking to develop plants which will capture sunlight with greater efficiency, use less water, and at the same time produce more abundantly. Once the schedule of irrigation is programmed, a single experienced central pivot operator can take care of at least ten fields.

This computerization of irrigation farming is not only stimulating to read about, it widens and deepens our perception of the new landscape by taking us below the surface, as it were; and the technological and financial infrastructure is precisely what should give us concern. The enormous investment in engineering, in equipment, in servicing, and maintaining each operation means that this kind of irrigation is at present well beyond the reach of the average landowning farmer. In his book on American agriculture, Walter Ebeling quotes a farm manager as saying that he had made a New Jersey investor in central pivot systems in Nebraska a millionaire.[1] And while this kind of sprinkler irrigation actually uses less water per acre than the traditional ditch irrigation, it has become so general in certain sections of the High Plains that it is only a matter of time before some wells run dry, and when that happens we will see round fields not of green but of a desolate gray.

Still, as air travelers, as amateur viewers of the landscape, our role is simply to look at the visible results of these projects and problems and to postpone the passing of ecological or social judgment until all the evidence is in. Americans are capable of seeing the dangers ahead and of trying to circumvent them. We can learn to breed and grow plants which use less water; we can also devise smaller and less expensive central pivot systems and other types of sprinklers. When tractors were introduced into American agriculture they were huge and costly and seemed to spell the doom of the small American farmer. Instead, they became small and inexpensive and versatile. A sustained interest in this landscape should eventually lead us to look for signs of change in the panorama below us. Already by looking closely, we can observe that the perfectly circular field of 130 acres of greenery has in many places begun to reach out and occupy some of the hitherto neglected corners which the rotating pipe could not reach. Eventually we will see square fields, and that, I think, from the spectator's point of view, will be a loss.

In the meantime we would do well to recall that newer definition of a landscape—an organization of man-made spaces—and with an artist's eye interpret what we see. Obviously we are looking down on what must be the most artificial, the most minutely planned and controlled agricultural landscape in America. But artificiality to a greater or less extent is part of every landscape, and what we should also note is that this kind of irrigation requires little or no modification of the topography. That in fact is why sprinkler irrigation is popular in the High Plains: the countryside is sufficiently rolling and uneven to make the digging of ditches and the watering of the surface a difficult if not an impossible task. The water, therefore, comes in the form of artificial rain and this rain, if moderate enough, sinks into the ground, no matter how uneven the surface. So these definitely artificial fields—artificial in form, artificial in content—merely lie on the surface and represent no permanent topographical change. Unlike the irrigated fields in the older landscape—bulldozed, leveled, sliced and scarred by ditches—these round fields can be abandoned without leaving a trace, just as traditional fields eventually revert to second growth and wilderness. In time we will see this happen again.

Perhaps the most significant feature of this High Plains landscape is the extraordinary self-sufficiency, the autonomy and functional isolation of each of these innumerable green circles; like billiard balls, they barely touch their neighbors, and nothing except propinquity seems to relate them one to another. Each grows its own crop according to its own individual schedule, each depends for its survival not on a common (or communal) supply of water or on a common tradition of farming or even on a common weather pattern, but solely on its own individual supply coming from its own well. We are confronted with the realization that these are not fields in the accepted sense of the word; these are areas or spaces rigidly defined by an influence or power emanating from a central source. Such is the scientific use of the word *field*, but we must now use it in discussing a farm landscape: the central agent of course is the pump, or the flow of water it produces, and these are fields of energy, for once given visible form.

It is surely a development of some significance when an ancient and familiar word begins to shift in definition, for it suggests that many other commonly accepted features of the landscape are likewise undergoing transformation. It would be foolish to attach too much importance to the development of a new and perhaps short-lived type of irrigation landscape. At the same time, it would be more than foolish to discount the many changes which have taken place over the last generations. And these changes are not merely a matter of shape and scale in the landscape, evident in the mile after mile of identical discs of green, slipping by beneath us like items on an assembly line, nor even a matter of the invisible power of computers to change the microclimate and the growth of plants. The real change is in ourselves and how we see the world. Flight has given us new eyes, and we are using them to discover a new order of spaces, new landscapes wherever we look.

Concluding with Landscapes

Southeastern Utah. (Photo: author)

Often a disconcerting thought has come to me and given me pause. It is this: Whatever I may have fondly supposed, all that I have been writing and saying over the past years has in the last analysis dealt with a single topic—how to define (or redefine) the concept *landscape*. The *concept;* not landscape as phenomena, as environments; these I have been able to handle without much difficulty. What everyone likes to hear is that the landscape where they live is unique of its kind, worthy of the closest study, and so one has only to emphasize its *unique* characteristics to give full satisfaction. Yet an unforeseen complication has arisen. The greater the number of landscapes I explored, the more it seemed that they all had traits in common and that the essence of each was not its uniqueness but its similarity to others. It occurred to me that there might be such a thing as a prototypal landscape, or more precisely landscape as a primordial idea, of which all these visible landscapes were merely so many imperfect manifestations. It then became a question of defining that idea or concept, after which the defining of the individual landscape would be plain sailing.

I cannot say that many others in the field of environmental studies have shared this perplexity of mine—a perplexity which any medieval monk could have disposed of in short order. I have been given to understand that the problem had been more than adequately handled by geographers and an-thropologists, and that it would be far better if I were concerned with the landscape itself—particularly the contemporary American landscape, much in need of criticism and reform. That may well have been good advice. Yet when we use a word carelessly (as we now use the word *landscape*) we are likely to get into trouble; and it is always prudent to know what we are talking about.

I have mentioned more than once how unsatisfactory we all find the current dictionary definition of the word: "A view or vista of scenery on the land, or a painting depicting such a scene." The formula dates back more than three hundred years. But since then we have learned to see a landscape as something more than beautiful scenery. We have learned that it can be designed and created from scratch, that it can grow old and fall into decay. We have ceased to think of it as remote from our daily lives, and indeed we now believe that to be part of a landscape, to derive our identity from it is an essential precondition of our being-in-the-world, in the most solemn meaning of the phrase. It is this greatly expanded significance of landscape that makes a new definition so necessary now.

In time we will doubtless formulate one. What we have recently come up with, in default of help from the dictionary, is something admittedly make-shift and incomplete. By rejecting the strictly esthetic or phenomenological approach—landscape as an isolated phenomenon stripped of origins and functions, unrelated to existence—we are able to discuss it in mundane terms, and it is not uncommon to hear a landscape referred to as the expression in terms of space of a given social order, a kind of two-dimensional language

147

with its own grammar and its own logic. The simile may lack precision; just the same, those who use it find it full of useful suggestions. Like a language, a landscape will have obscure and undecipherable origins, like a language it is the slow creation of all elements in society. It grows according to its own laws, rejecting or accepting neologisms as it sees fit, clinging to obsolescent forms, inventing new ones. A landscape, like a language, is the field of perpetual conflict and compromise between what is established by authority and what the vernacular insists upon preferring. Like the grammarian or the lexicographer, the planner, the reformer has to take a stand, and it is usually on the side of what is rational and correct, on the side of the intellectual establishment. That is as it should be. We are familiar enough with the tyranny a too highly structured language or a landscape too carefully planned can exert, but there is something to be said for rules, however arbitrary. Just as a language without established standards of elegance and clarity and re- spect for tradition can thwart the best of minds, a landscape left to itself without long-range goals, without structure, without law, though it may call itself a paradise, ends by frustrating any search for social or moral order.

The comparison can be carried just so far, but in the case of both language and landscape, growth and preservation and beauty is finally, I think, a matter of history and how we deal with it. Whatever definition of landscape we finally reach, to be serviceable it will have to take into account the cease- less interaction between the ephemeral, the mobile, the vernacular on the one hand, and the authority of legally established, premeditated permanent forms on the other.

It may be that I am here on the track of that elusive landscape concept: the ideal landscape defined not as a static utopia dedicated to ecological or social or religious principles, but as an environment where permanence and change have struck a balance. Few landscapes have achieved this and fewer still have managed to maintain it for any length of time. But all of them, it seems to me, have sought it; all of them in one manner or another, that is to say, have acknowledged the existence of landscape as idea. The world being what it is, it is far easier to find examples of imbalance than of landscape balance. The two examples of the former I offer are worth studying not merely for their cautionary value—for one shows the perils of mobility, the other the perils which come with too great a regard for *position* in the landscape—but also because they are both related, though indirectly, to our own American land- scape and its future.

I have elsewhere explained the original meaning of the word *landscape,* so it is enough to say that it meant a collection, a "sheaf" of lands, presumably interrelated and part of a system. A land was a defined piece of ground, and we can assume that in the medieval world it was most often used to indicate a patch of plowed or cultivated ground, that being the most valuable kind. Landscape therefore must have been a word much used by villagers and peasants and farmhands; it described their own small world. But how much was it used by other elements in society? It rarely occurs in legal documents of the period. The Domesday Book, a remarkable inventory of land holdings compiled by order of William the Conqueror in the eleventh century, was, to be sure, written in Latin, but no translation ever mentioned landscape, and indeed the word itself seems to have fallen into disuse. Two centuries after the conquest a new term, imported from France, though of Latin origin, took its place. *Country* or *countryside* came to indicate a much more extensive, though less precisely defined area: the territory of a community of people all speaking the same dialect, all engaged in the same kind of farming, all subjects of the same local lord, all conscious of having customs and traditions of their own and of possessing certain ancient rights and privileges. It was not until modern times that the word *country* came to indicate *nation*.

It is here, in the usage of the two words *landscape* and *country,* that we are confronted with the distinction between the vernacular and the aristocratic or political concepts of space. In the view of the noblemen and clergy, of the larger landowners, *landscape* was merely a vernacular or peasant term describing a cluster of small, temporary, crudely measured spaces which frequently changed hands and even changed in shape and size. It was, in fact, a fragment of a larger feudal estate, a right or series of rights granted to its occupants but ultimately the property of the lord or of the crown. It was a term current only in small villages. The aristocratic concept of space was entirely different. The estate of a nobleman or of a bishop, the barony or domain of the knight, the forest of the king, not to mention his kingdom, all had a definite, almost sacred origin, their boundaries vouched for by treaty or charter. Those who held them not only had the right to administer justice, but to bequeath them to their descendants. Aristocratic space, in the medieval world, was thus permanent and relatively autonomous. It was the creation of political or legal decisions.

Although the two kinds of space were intermingled, the difference between the two ways of seeing the world and of organizing space was profound, and insofar as we are exploring the early usage of the word *landscape* it is the *vernacular* landscape which concerns us. The current tendency to associate the word *vernacular* with a local form of speech and a local form of art and decoration entitles us to use the word to describe other aspects of local culture. The word derives from the Latin *verna,* meaning a slave born in the house of his or her master, and by extension in Classical times it meant a native, one whose existence was confined to a village or estate and who was devoted to routine work. A vernacular culture would imply a way of life ruled by tradition and custom, entirely remote from the larger world of politics and law; a way of life where identity derived not from permanent possession of land but from membership in a group or super-family.

It follows, I think, that there can be such a thing as a vernacular landscape:

one where evidences of a political organization of space are largely or entirely absent. I have already mentioned several features of the political landscape: the visibility and sanctity of boundaries, the importance of monuments and of centrifugal highways, the close relationship between status and enclosed space. By *political* I mean those spaces and structures designed to impose or preserve a unity and order on the land, or in keeping with a long-range, large-scale plan. Under that heading we should include such modern features as the interstate highway, the hydroelectric dam, the airport and power transmission lines, whether we happen to care for them or not.

A vernacular landscape reveals a distinct way of defining and handling time and space. In the United States there is a series of vernacular landscapes of a particularly pure type in the Pueblo Indian communities of the Southwest, and whenever we see one we are likely to find it confusing and all but impossible to interpret in our conventional European–American terms. The medieval landscape is scarcely easier to understand, even though in the course of centuries it gradually acquired several political components: castles, manors, king's highways, and chartered cities. These are what enable us to see its evolution. Yet underneath those symbols of permanent political power there lay a vernacular landscape—or rather thousands of small and impoverished vernacular landscapes, organizing and using spaces in their traditional way and living in communities governed by custom, held together by personal relationships. We learn something about them by investigating the topographical and technological and social factors which determined their economy and their way of life, but in the long run I suspect no landscape, vernacular or otherwise, can be comprehended unless we perceive it as an organization of space; unless we ask ourselves who owns or uses the spaces, how they were created and how they change. Often it is the legal aspects of the landscape that give us the clearest insight, especially into the relationship between the peasant or villager and the piece of land he works.

"It is very rare, during the whole of the feudal era," Marc Bloch remarks,

> for anyone to speak of ownership, either of an estate or an office. . . . [T]he word ownership as applied to landed property would have been almost meaningless . . . for nearly all land and a great many human beings were burdened at this time with a multiplicity of obligations differing in their nature, but all apparently of equal merit. None implied the fixed proprietary exclusiveness which belonged to the concept of ownership in Roman law. The tenant who—from father to son, as a rule—ploughs the land and gathers in the crop; his immediate lord to whom he pays dues and who, in certain circumstances, can resume possession of the land; the lord of the lord, and so on, right up the feudal ladder—how many persons there are who can say, each with as much justification as the other "that is my field!"[1]

Spaces in this vernacular landscape thus indicate personal relationships, and they indicate in no less complicated manner the involved and often conflicting traditions of the community: who controls the vast number of "waste spaces"—some as extensive as a whole moor or marsh, others no larger than the margin of a road or a lane. Is the road itself a waste? Given a new use, a space changes its name: a "land" grown to grass becomes a "ley"; waste, preempted by the crown, becomes a royal forest with its own set of laws. Maitland, the legal historian, endeavoring to make legal sense of the landscape of medieval Cambridge, reminds us of its hopeless complexity and bids us "think of the grantor [King John] and his royal rights, of the grantees and their complex interests, of the strips in the fields and the odds and ends of sward, of the green commons of the town, of the house covered nucleus . . . of the patchwork of fiefs, the network of rents"[2]—and from this confusion we are somehow to deduce a coherent spatial pattern.

At the present state of our studies of the vernacular landscape as a type all that we can say is that its spaces are usually small, irregular in shape, subject to rapid change in use, in ownership, in dimensions; that the houses, even the villages themselves, grow, shrink, change morphology, change location; that there is always a vast amount of "common land"—waste, pasturage, forest, areas where natural resources are exploited in a piecemeal manner; that its roads are little more than paths and lanes, never maintained and rarely permanent; finally that the vernacular landscape is a scattering of hamlets and clusters of fields, islands in a sea of waste or wilderness changing from generation to generation, leaving no monuments, only abandonment or signs of renewal.

Mobility and change are the key to the vernacular landscape, but of an involuntary, reluctant sort; not the expression of restlessness and search for improvement but an unending patient adjustment to circumstances. Far too often these are the arbitrary decisions of those in power, but natural conditions play their part and so do ignorance and a blind loyalty to local ways, and so does the absence of long-range objectives: the absence of what we would call a sense of future history. A vernacular landscape, both in the Southwest and in medieval Europe, is an impressive display of devotion to common customs and of an inexhaustible ingenuity in finding short-term solutions.

At the same time we cannot overlook what to us is the cultural poverty of such a landscape, its lack of any purposeful continuity. It thinks not of history but of legends and myths. Well into the Renaissance and even later, the inhabitants of vernacular landscapes in Europe still half-believed in heathen divinities, adorned their houses with heathen symbols, and observed heathen rites and holidays. Even historical figures, like Charlemagne or Barbarossa, historical events like the Crusades or the actual settlement of a town or city, were transformed into fairy tales. They lived in a landscape of ancient villages, ruined castles, churches built on the site of temples, yet the only monuments they recognized were miraculous springs, magic rocks, and trees, the only event they understood was the sound of Odin with his pack of hounds rushing through the forest by night. A landscape without visible signs of political history is a landscape without memory or forethought. We are inclined in America to think that the value of monuments is simply to remind us of origins. They are much more valuable as reminders of long-range, collective purpose, of goals and objectives and principles. As such even the least sightly of monuments gives a landscape beauty and dignity and keeps the collective memory alive.

Let us call that early medieval landscape Landscape One. There is another landscape (which we may call Landscape Two), which began to take shape in the latter part of the fifteenth century and which we can associate with the Renaissance; and since we are giving them names, let us identify a Landscape Three, which we can see in certain aspects of contemporary America.

I am tempted to think that Landscape Three is already beginning to show some of the characteristics of Landscape One, but before I offer evidence let me say something about Landscape Two, which was in many ways the reverse of Landscape One. We are in fact very familiar with Landscape Two. Artists and architects and landscape designers spend much time studying it, and they copy it in their professional work; and all of us who write about it travel to Europe to see it at firsthand. So I merely mention the ways in which it differs from Landscape One. Its spaces, rural and urban, are clearly and permanently defined and made visible by walls and hedges or zones of open greenery or lawn. They are designed to be self-contained and shapely and beautiful. Landscape Two sets great score on visibility; that is why we have that seventeenth-century definition of landscape as "a vista or view of scenery of the land"—landscape as a work of art, as a kind of supergarden. Unlike Landscape One, which mixed all kinds of uses and spaces together, Landscape Two insists on spaces which are homogenous and devoted to a single purpose. It makes a distinction between city and country, between forest and field, between public and private, rich and poor, work and play; it prefers the linear frontier between nations rather than the medieval patchwork of intermingled territories. As for the distinction between mobility and immobility, it clearly believes that whatever is temporary or short-lived or movable is not to be encouraged.

But the essential characteristic of Landscape Two is its belief in the sanctity of *place*. It is place, permanent position both in the social and topographical sense, that gives us our identity. The function of space according to this belief is to make us visible, allow us to put down roots and become members of society. Land in Landscape One meant being a member of a working community; it was a temporary symbol of relationships. In Landscape Two land means property and permanence and power.

Landscape Two started to evolve at a time in European history when the old customary farm community with its disposable parcels of land and its confusion of rights and obligations was being abandoned in favor of the individual ownership and operation of farms: private holdings composed of single-purpose permanent fields with the homestead of the owner in the center of the property. This was a time when men were discovering the natural environment and its many variations in climate and soil and topography, and when the challenge to agriculture was to define all varieties of land and put them to their appropriate use. It was in consequence a time when the forest was discovered as a distinct environment, with distinct economic and ecological characteristics; an environment worth preserving and improving.

There is little new to be said about the beauty and order of Landscape Two. It remains to this day the most successful landscape, esthetically speaking, that there has ever been in the Western world, one which we will always try to imitate when we want to produce landscapes for delight and inspiration. Americans have a special reason for admiring it, for it is here in the United States that we see the largest and most impressive example of neo-classic spatial organization. Our national grid system, devised by the Founding Fathers, represents the last attempt to produce a Classical political landscape, one based on the notion that certain spaces—notably the square and the rectangle—were inherently beautiful and therefore suited to the creation of a just society. It is, to be sure, a landscape with few dramatic beauties and much monotony, but it is a landscape which conforms to Winckelmann's definition of Classical perfection: one of noble simplicity and quiet grandeur.

What we enjoy about the early-nineteenth-century American landscape is the ease with which it can be read and interpreted. The farm stands in the midst of its fields and clearly reveals its degree of prosperity and contentment. Each church has a white steeple, each public square has a monument, each field its fence, each straight road its destination. It is a landscape of rectangular fields, green woodlands, white houses, and red brick towns. It is like a luminous painting: vivid, carefully composed, appealing to the emotions, and reassuringly stable.

Yet it did not last for long: scarcely a half century, and a number of reasons can be given for its rapid decay: the coming of the railroad, the opening up of newer land further West, the invention of the balloon frame and of horse-drawn farm equipment, the growth of manufacturing in the East, the influx of settlers from Europe—all these developments affected the spatial organization of Landscape Two in America and in a few decades made it obsolete. Yet I cannot help feeling that even from the start Landscape Two was not entirely suited to us. It never produced those politically active farm communities that Jefferson and his colleagues dreamt of, never really persuaded us to put down roots and stay put in one place. Instead of being a blueprint for the ideal Classical democratic social order, the grid system became simply an easy and effective way of dividing up the land and of encouraging the settlement of the Midwest. The question which we will eventually have to confront is whether

Landscape Two ever belonged in the English-speaking New World. (I say *English-speaking* advisedly, because it *did* take hold in Latin America.)

The settlement of Anglo-Americans can best be understood as a belated episode in the history of Landscape One: a last titanic wave of mobility, of immigrants leaving the vanishing vernacular landscape of rural England. Once settled here, the predominantly young, blue-collar population produced a colonial version of Landscape One—but lacking in one important traditional feature: the farm village. New England tried to produce it, the authorities in London tried to produce it in Virginia, but new ways of farming, new kinds of land ownership, and a new kind of freedom frustrated every attempt, and by the time of the Revolution even in New England the farm village was out of date. What survived of that early colonial vernacular culture was its mobility, its adaptability, its preference for the transitory, the ephemeral: the short-lived log cabins, the brief exploitation of the environment; the ad hoc community of the frontier and the trading post, even while the grid of Landscape Two stood waiting for Jefferson's Classical farm villages to appear.

It would be wrong to imply that modern America is entirely the product of that vernacular culture, or that we do not possess a vast and rich landscape, urban as well as rural, dedicated to stability and history and established landscape values. My concern is that these two landscapes do not always recognize what each has to offer to the other and that Landscape Three may fail to achieve a balance between them. I do not believe that the Establishment—political, intellectual, artistic—is aware of the vitality and extent of that vernacular element, and I do not believe that we recognize the danger of having two distinct sublandscapes, one dedicated to stability and place, the other dedicated to mobility. Such was the case in Landscape One. Our vernacular landscape has unparalleled vitality and diversity, but it resembles Landscape One in its detachment from formal space, its indifference to history, and its essentially utilitarian, conscienceless use of the environment. We cannot say that we are returning to the Dark Ages, but the similarity between Landscape Three and Landscape One is based on an important circumstance: both lack the humanist tradition of the Renaissance. Both are ignorant of Landscape Two and what it stood for.

As I travel about the country, I am often bewildered by the proliferation of spaces and the uses of spaces that had no counterpart in the traditional landscape: parking lots, landing fields, shopping centers, trailer courts, high-rise condominiums, wildlife shelters, Disneyland. I am bewildered by our casual use of space: churches used as discotheques, dwellings used as churches, downtown streets used for jogging, empty lots in crowded cities, industrial plants in the open country, cemeteries used for archery practice, Easter sunrise services in a football stadium. I am confused by the temporary spaces

I see: the drive-in, fast-food establishments that are torn down after a year, the fields planted to corn and then to soya beans and then subdivided; the trailer communities that vanish when vacation time is over, the tropical gardens in shopping malls that are replaced each season; motels abandoned when the highway moves. Because of my age my first reaction to these new spaces is dismay; they are not the kind of spaces I was accustomed to in the Landscape Two of my youth. But my second and (I hope) more tolerant reaction is that all this is part of our culture, that it can be treated with respect and that here is a new and challenging field of environmental design.

I would like to think that in the future the profession of landscape architecture will expand beyond its present confines (established by Landscape Two) and involve itself in making mobility orderly and beautiful. This would mean knowing a great deal about land, its uses, its values, and the political and economic and cultural forces affecting its distribution. The environmental designer should be concerned with the spatial changes taking place. It is precisely in the field of land use and community planning that a trained imagination, an awareness of environment and habitat can be of the greatest value. What has been done in the way of producing new landscapes, new wilderness areas, farms and factories and cities in Holland and Israel could serve as a model. Environmental design is not simply a matter of protecting nature as it is, but of creating a new nature, a new beauty. It is finally a matter of defining landscape in a way that includes both the mobility of the vernacular and the political infrastructure of a stable social order.

In matters having to do with the natural environment we are most of us children of Landscape Two. From that parent we have learned not only to study the world around us but also to lavish care upon it and bring it to a state of lasting perfection. It was Landscape Two that taught us that the contemplation of nature can be a kind of revelation of the invisible world, and of ourselves.

But it was also Landscape Two that impressed upon us the notion that there can be only *one* kind of landscape: a landscape identified with a very static, very conservative social order, and that there can be only one true philosophy of nature: that of Landscape Two.

That first heritage of love and wonder is still with us, stronger perhaps than ever. It is that other heritage, that clinging to obsolete forms and attitudes, that threatens the emergence of a truly balanced Landscape Three. We no longer live in the country, we no longer farm, we no longer derive our identity from possession of land. Like the harassed peasant of Landscape One, though to a far greater degree, we derive our identity from our relationship with other people, and when we talk about the importance of *place,* the necessity of belonging to a *place,* let us be clear that in Landscape Three place means the people in it, not simply the natural environment. For political and economic reasons Landscape Two greatly exaggerated the importance of belonging to a community. But the agricultural community was what was meant, the tightly organized hierarchy of landowners and masters and workers. Not every applicant was admitted, and the conditions attached to membership were strict and arbitrary; final acceptance was slow in coming. In Landscape Three the reverse is the case, and the ease with which a stranger can be assimilated, the speed with which a new community can come into being are both extraordinary phenomena. It may not be entirely accurate to say (as a developer once said to me) that "people follow plumbing," meaning that utilities are the infrastructure of any residential community. It is nevertheless true that we have abandoned the old political procedures of creating places. The forming of a new community now calls for little more than the gregarious impulse of a dozen families attracted by certain elementary public services. This is the kind of new community that we are seeing all over America: at remote construction sites, in recreation areas, in trailer courts, in the shanty towns of wetbacks and migrant workers; the emergence of what we may call vernacular communities—without political status, without plan, ruled by informal local custom, often ingenious adaptations to an unlikely site and makeshift materials, destined to last no more than a year or two, and working as well as most communities do. They would be better and last longer if they were properly designed and serviced. They could acquire dignity if the political landscape made a gesture of recognition. Yet very little is needed to give those new communities a true identity: a reminder, a symbol of permanence to indicate that they too have a history ahead of them.

One reason for paying more attention to this aspect of Landscape Three is that these settlements will in time serve as nuclei for small-scale landscapes. For that is always how landscapes have been formed; not only by topography and political decisions, but by the indigenous organization and development of spaces to serve the needs of the focal community: gainful employment, recreation, social contacts, contacts with nature, contacts with the alien world. In one form or another, these are the ends which all landscapes serve, and that is why they are all fundamentally versions of the primal *idea* of landscape.

My search for a definition has led me back to that old Anglo-Saxon meaning: landscape is not scenery, it is not a political unit; it is really no more than a collection, a system of man-made spaces on the surface of the earth. Whatever its shape or size it is *never* simply a natural space, a feature of the natural environment; it is *always* artificial, always synthetic, always subject to sudden or unpredictable change. We create them and need them because every landscape is the place where we establish our own human organization of space and time. It is where the slow, natural processes of growth and maturity and decay are deliberately set aside and history is substituted. A landscape is where we speed up or retard or divert the cosmic program and impose our own. "By conquering nature," Mircea Eliade writes, "man can become Nature's rival without being the slave of time. . . . Science and industry proclaim that man can achieve things better and faster than nature if he, by means of his intelligence, succeeds in penetrating to her secrets."[3]

When we see how we have succeeded in imposing our own rhythm on nature in the agricultural landscape, how we have altered the life cycle of plants and animals and even transposed the seasons, we become aware of how dangerous a role we have assumed, and there are many who say that the salvation of Landscape Three depends on our relinquishing this power to alter the flow of time and on our returning to a more natural order. But the new ordering of time should affect not only nature, it should affect ourselves. It promises us a new kind of history, a new, more responsive social order, and ultimately a new landscape.

Notes

The Word Itself

1. Kenneth Clark, *Landscape Into Painting* (New York, 1950), p. 140.
2. H. L. Gray, *English Field Systems* (Cambridge, 1915), p. 19.

A Pair of Ideal Landscapes

1. Fustel de Coulanges, *The Ancient City* (New York, 1956), pp. 62ff.
2. Thucydides, *The History of the Peloponnesian War* 1. 139.
3. Arnold Toynbee, *A Study of History*, vol. 5 (Oxford, 1939), p. 594.
4. R. E. Wycherley, *How the Greeks Built Cities* (New York, 1969), p. 72.
5. Aristotle, *Politics* 7.11.
6. Venturi, *Learning from Las Vegas* (New York, 1976), p. 6.
7. Jean-Pierre Vernant, *Mythe et pensée chez les Grecs* (Paris, 1965), p. 154.
8. W. H. Whyte, "Small Space is Beautiful," *Technology Review* (July 1982).
9. John Bradford, *Ancient Landscapes: Studies in Field Archaeology* (London, 1957), p. 156.
10. Ferdinando Castagnoli, *Orthogonal Town Planning in Antiquity* (Cambridge, 1971), p. 73.
11. Ibid., p. 121.
12. Plato, *Laws* 5.9.
13. Aristotle, *Politics* 4.6.
14. Ibid., 6.4
15. John Ruskin, *Modern Painters*, vol. 3, pp. 234ff.
16. John Fraser Hart, *The Look of the Land* (Englewood Cliffs, N.J., 1975), p. 77.
17. Norman J. G. Pounds, *An Historical Geography of Europe* (Cambridge, England, 1972), p. 57.
18. Oswald Spengler, *The Decline of the West*, vol. 1 (New York, 1939), p. 176.
19. Wycherley, *How the Greeks Built Cities*, p. 42.
20. Plato, *Laws* 6.
21. Arnim von Gerkan, "Grenzen und Grössen der vierzehn Regionen Roms," 1949.
22. William Ernest Hocking, "A Philosophy of Life for the American Farmer (and others)," in *Yearbook of Agriculture 1940*, p. 1064.
23. H. Cavailles, *La Route Francaise* (Paris, 1935), p. 119.
24. Hamilton A. Tyler, *Pueblo Gods and Myths* (Norman, Okla., 1964), p. 105.
25. Mircea Eliade, "La Terre-mère et les Hierogamies cosmiques," *Eranos Jahrbuch* (1953).
26. Gladys A. Reichard, *Navaho Religion* (Princeton, 1963), p. 49.
27. Ferdinand Tönnies, *Community and Society*, ed. C. P. Loomis (East Lansing, 1957), p. 206.
28. Jacob Grimm, *Deutsche rechtsalterthümer*, vol. 2 (Göttingen, 1828), p. 8.
29. Georges Duby, *L'économie rurale et la vie des campagnes*, vol. 1 (Paris, 1962), p. 71.
30. Richard Krebner, "The Settlement and Colonization of Europe," in *The Cambridge Economic History*, vol. 1 (1942), p. 20.
31. H. C. Darby, ed., *A New Historical Geography of England* (Cambridge, 1973), p. 55.
32. A. Schwappach, *Handbuch der Forst und Jagdgeschichte*, vol. 1 (Leipzig, 1888), p. 40.

33. H. P. R. Finberg, ed., *The Agrarian History of England and Wales,* vol. 1, pt. 2 (London, 1972), p. 406.
34. Marc Bloch, *Feudal Society,* trans. L. A. Manyon, vol. 1 (Chicago, 1961), p. 6.
35. Fernand Braudel, *The Structures of Everyday Life* (New York, 1981), p. 276.
36. Ruskin, *Modern Painters,* vol. 3, p. 246.
37. Ruth Benedict, *Patterns of Culture* (New York, 1938), pp. 116ff.
38. Jacob Grimm, *Teutonic Mythology,* vol. 2, trans. James S. Stallybrass (1883; repr. New York, 1966), p. 517.

Country Towns for a New Part of the Country

1. E. T. Price, "The Central Courthouse Square," *The Geographical Review* (January 1968).
2. Clifton Johnson, *Highways and Byways of the South* (New York, 1904), pp. 76ff.

The Movable Dwelling and How It Came to America

1. Simone Roux, *La Maison dans l'histoire* (Paris, 1976), p. 171.
2. Alan Gowans, *Images of American Living* (Philadelphia, 1964), pp. 3ff.
3. Philip Alexander Bruce, *Economic History of Virginia in the Seventeenth Century,* vol. 2 (New York, 1895), p. 543.
4. Thomas Jefferson, *Notes on the State of Virginia* (London, 1787), p. 145.
5. Dianne Tebbetts, "Traditional Houses of Independence County, Arkansas," *Pioneer America* 10 (1978).
6. George A. Stokes, "Lumbering and Western Louisiana Cultural Landscape."

Stone and Its Substitutes

1. *The Apocryphal New Testament,* trans. M. R. James (Oxford, 1923), pp. 364ff.
2. Mircea Eliade, *The Forge and the Crucible* (New York, 1962), p. 171.
3. W. R. Lethaby, *Architecture, Mysticism, and Myth* (1891: repr. New York, 1975), p. 5.
4. Eliade, *The Forge and the Crucible,* pp. 43ff.
5. Gaston Bachelard, *La Terre et les Reveries de la Volonté,* (Paris, 1948), pp. 240, 258.
6. Peter Fingesten, *The Eclipse of Symbolism* (Columbia, S.C., 1970), p. 75.
7. Hans Sedlmayr, *Die Enstehung der Kathedrale* (Zurich, 1950), p. 84.

Craftsman Style and Technostyle

1. Faber Birren, *Color in Your World* (New York, 1962), p. 59.

The Origin of Parks

1. *Garden and Forest,* no. 373 (April 1895), p. 152.

A Vision of New Fields

1. Walter Ebeling, *The Fruited Plain* (Berkeley, 1979), p. 253.

Concluding with Landscapes

1. Bloch, *Feudal Society,* vol. 1, p. 116.
2. F. W. Maitland, *Township and Borough* (Cambridge, 1898), p. 81.
3. Eliade, *The Forge and the Crucible,* p. 169.

Index